INCREDIBLE ENGLISH

Activity Book 4

Peter Redpath

Sarah Phillips

OXFORD
UNIVERSITY PRESS

OXFORD
UNIVERSITY PRESS

Great Clarendon Street, Oxford OX2 6DP

Oxford University Press is a department of the University of Oxford.
It furthers the University's objective of excellence in research, scholarship,
and education by publishing worldwide in

Oxford New York

Auckland Cape Town Dar es Salaam Hong Kong Karachi
Kuala Lumpur Madrid Melbourne Mexico City Nairobi
New Delhi Shanghai Taipei Toronto

With offices in

Argentina Austria Brazil Chile Czech Republic France Greece
Guatemala Hungary Italy Japan Poland Portugal Singapore
South Korea Switzerland Thailand Turkey Ukraine Vietnam

OXFORD and OXFORD ENGLISH are registered trade marks of
Oxford University Press in the UK and in certain other countries

© Oxford University Press 2007

The moral rights of the author have been asserted

Database right Oxford University Press (maker)

First published 2007

2018 2017 2016 2015 2014
 16   15   14   13

No unauthorized photocopying

All rights reserved. No part of this publication may be reproduced,
stored in a retrieval system, or transmitted, in any form or by any means,
without the prior permission in writing of Oxford University Press,
or as expressly permitted by law, or under terms agreed with the appropriate
reprographics rights organization. Enquiries concerning reproduction
outside the scope of the above should be sent to the ELT Rights Department,
Oxford University Press, at the address above

You must not circulate this book in any other binding or cover
and you must impose this same condition on any acquirer

Any websites referred to in this publication are in the public domain and
their addresses are provided by Oxford University Press for information only.
Oxford University Press disclaims any responsibility for the content

ISBN: 978 0 19 444016 5

Printed in China

ACKNOWLEDGEMENTS

Illustrations by: Kathy Baxendale pp 20, 21, 75, 80, 94; Adrian Barclay pp 10, 11, 30, 33, 40, 41, 71, 81, 90, 91; Garry Parsons (songs) pp 10, 20, 30, 40, 50, 60, 70, 80, 90; Mark Ruffle p 96; Jo Taylor/Sylvie Poggio pp 13, 15, 16, 17, 24, 25, 26, 27, 29, 31, 33, 35, 36, 37, 43, 55, 56, 57, 60, 65, 73, 76, 87, 95; Matt Ward/Beehive Illustration pp 4, 6, 7, 8, 9, 14, 17, 18, 23, 24, 26, 27, 34, 38, 39, 44, 46, 47, 48, 53, 54, 55, 58, 63, 64, 66, 67, 68, 69, 74, 75, 77, 78, 79, 83, 84, 85, 86, 88, 89; Dave Whammond/Three in a Box pp 12, 22, 32, 42, 45, 50, 51, 52, 59, 62, 72, 82, 92.

Commissioned photography by: Gareth Boden pp 30, 31.

The Publishers would like to thank the following for their permission to reproduce photographs and other copyright material: Ardea pp 61 (peregrine falcon/John Daniels), 81 (Atlantic cod/Pat Morris), (pike/Brian Bevan), (stingray/Valerie Taylor), (brown trout/Pat Morris); Alamy pp 41 (Venus flytrap/Renee Morris), (edelweiss/Paroli Galperti), (fungus/John Martin), 48 (tiger/Imagebroker), (panda/Robert Pickett), 61 (Maglev train/Kevin Foy), (fighter plane/Transtock Inc), 70 (pyramid/Rolf Richardson), (pharaoh/Bygonetimes), (mummy/EddyButtarellie/CuboImages srl), 95 (snowmobile Alaska/Brian and Cherry Alexander), 96 (boy Turkey/Rebecca Erol), (girl Thailand/Cris Haigh); Corbis pp 70 (A god Khnum/Sandro Vannini), (Goddess Nephthys/Dallas and John Heaton/Free Agents Ltd); 91 (man making semaphore/Bettmann), (mirrors used to signal/Hulton Deutsch); Getty Images pp 61 (man running/Brad Wilson), 91 (Morse code operator/Meyer Pfund/Hulton Archive), 96 (boy Alaska/Frank Herholdt), (girl New Zealand/Seth Joel); Lonely Planet Images p 95 (NZ School bus/Jon Davison); Mary Evans Picture Library p 91 (Native Americans and smoke signals); Oxford Scientific Films pp 41 (strawberries/Botanica), 61 (mouse/Ifa Bilder team Gmbh), (bee/Paulo De Oliveira); OUP p 61 (cat).

INCREDIBLE ENGLISH

Activity Book

1	Playing outdoors	4
2	Art	14
3	Health	24
4	On the farm	34
5	Animal life	44
6	Safety	54
7	At school	64
8	Underwater life	74
9	Technology	84
	Children around the world	94

Peter Redpath

Sarah Phillips

1 Playing outdoors

1 Number the pictures. Then write.

1 climb   2 row   3 skateboard   4 fish
5 waterski   6 sail   7 rollerblade   8 play hide and seek

Activities with water	Activities without water

2 Listen and match. 1.3

What can you do?

4 Unit 1   Outdoor activities   Can you swim? Yes, I can.

3 Read and correct Archie's notes.

My week

Monday: go waterskiing or ~~play tennis~~
Tuesday: go rollerblading or play football
Wednesday: go rowing or go climbing
Thursday: play basketball or play tennis
Friday: go skateboarding or go swimming
Saturday: go fishing or go sailing
Sunday: play basketball or go rowing

THE INCREDIBLE ADVENTURE CAMP

Hello kids,

Welcome to the Incredible Adventure camp! There are lots of things to do.
You can play football on Monday or you can go waterskiing. You can go swimming on Tuesday and Friday. On Tuesday you can also go rollerblading. You can go sailing and climbing on Wednesday, and on Thursday you can play tennis or football. Friday is a big day! We have a swimming competition! On Saturday you can go fishing or skateboarding. On Sunday you can go rowing on the lake.
Have a good time!

Mr B Busy
The Activities Director

4 Write.

spelling

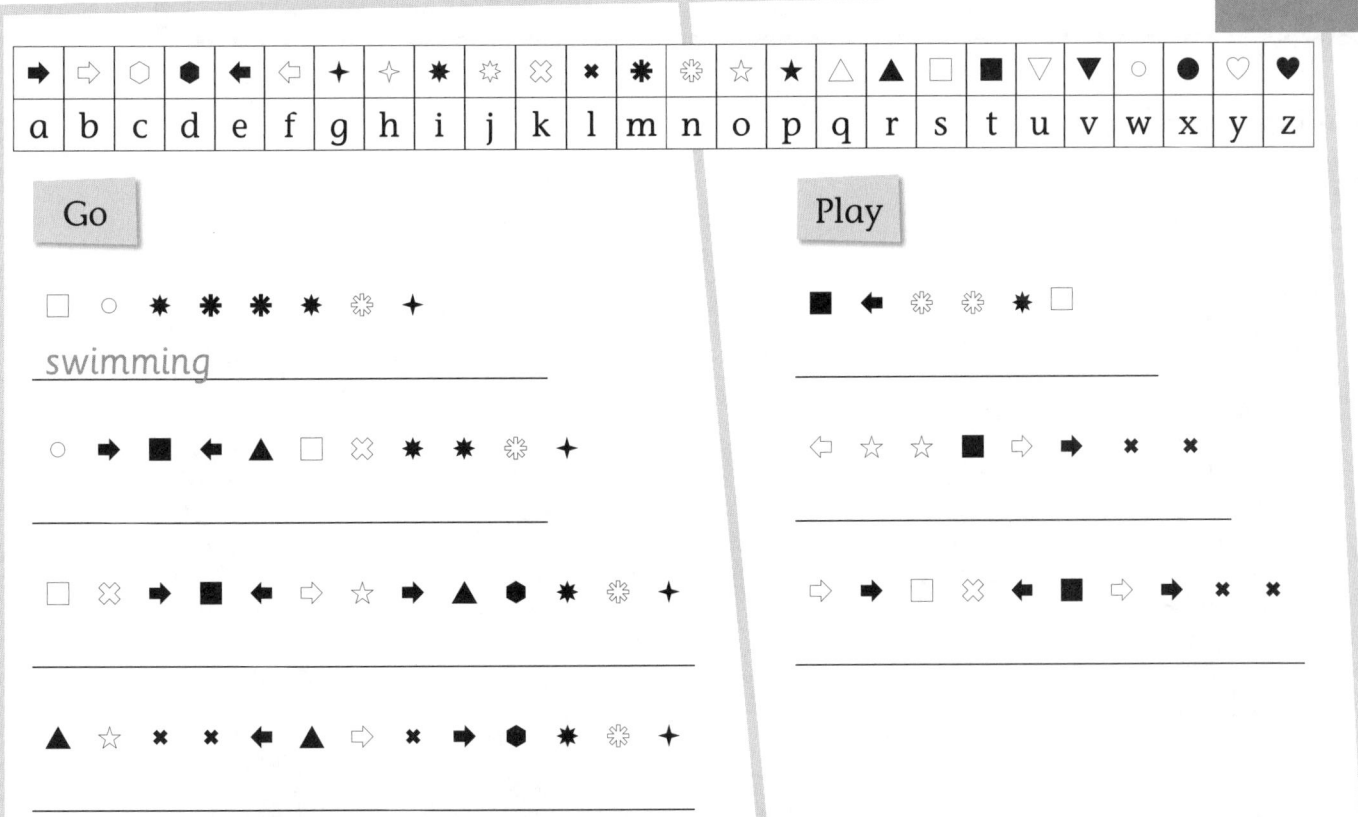

Go — swimming

Play

You can ... | Collocations with go / play

Unit 1 — 5

I want to | play tennis | . | I don't want to | go fishing | .

5 Write the sentences.

6 Listen and number. 1.6

7 Look and write.

Let's go sailing!   Let's go waterskiing!
Let's go rollerblading!
Let's go climbing!

Great idea!
No thanks, I don't want to go …

1. Let's go sailing! — Great idea!
2.
3.
4.

8 You're at the Incredible Adventure Camp! Write a dialogue.

◆ *Let's go swimming.*

Unit 1   7

9 Listen to the story again. 🔊 1.4

10 Write the words in groups.

play hide and seek   six o'clock   brilliant!
go fishing   fantastic!   play tennis   nine o'clock

Great!   five o'clock   go swimming

11 Choose words and complete the playscript. Act.

Archie:	Wake up! Let's _____
Eve:	Oh no… What time is it?
Molly:	It's _____ .
Luke:	Let's _____ .
Finn:	_____ !
Eve:	Oh… no.
Jazmin:	Eve, I want to _____ .
Archie:	I don´t want to _____ !
Eve:	Oh, I'm tired!
Molly:	Eve, can we _____ ?
Archie:	_____ !
Jazmin:	Sshh. She wants to read her book.
Eve:	Come on kids!
All:	Oh, Eve!
Eve:	It's _____ … let's _____ .
All:	Let's have a rest.

12 Read and order the sentences.

Emails

- Molly. ☐
- There are lots of things to do. ☐
- Dear Mum and Dad, [1]
- Every day I go sailing with Jazmin and I play basketball with Finn. ☐
- Love, ☐
- I'm having a great time at the Incredible Adventure Camp. ☐
- The food is very good – it's chicken for lunch today! ☐

13 Read and complete.

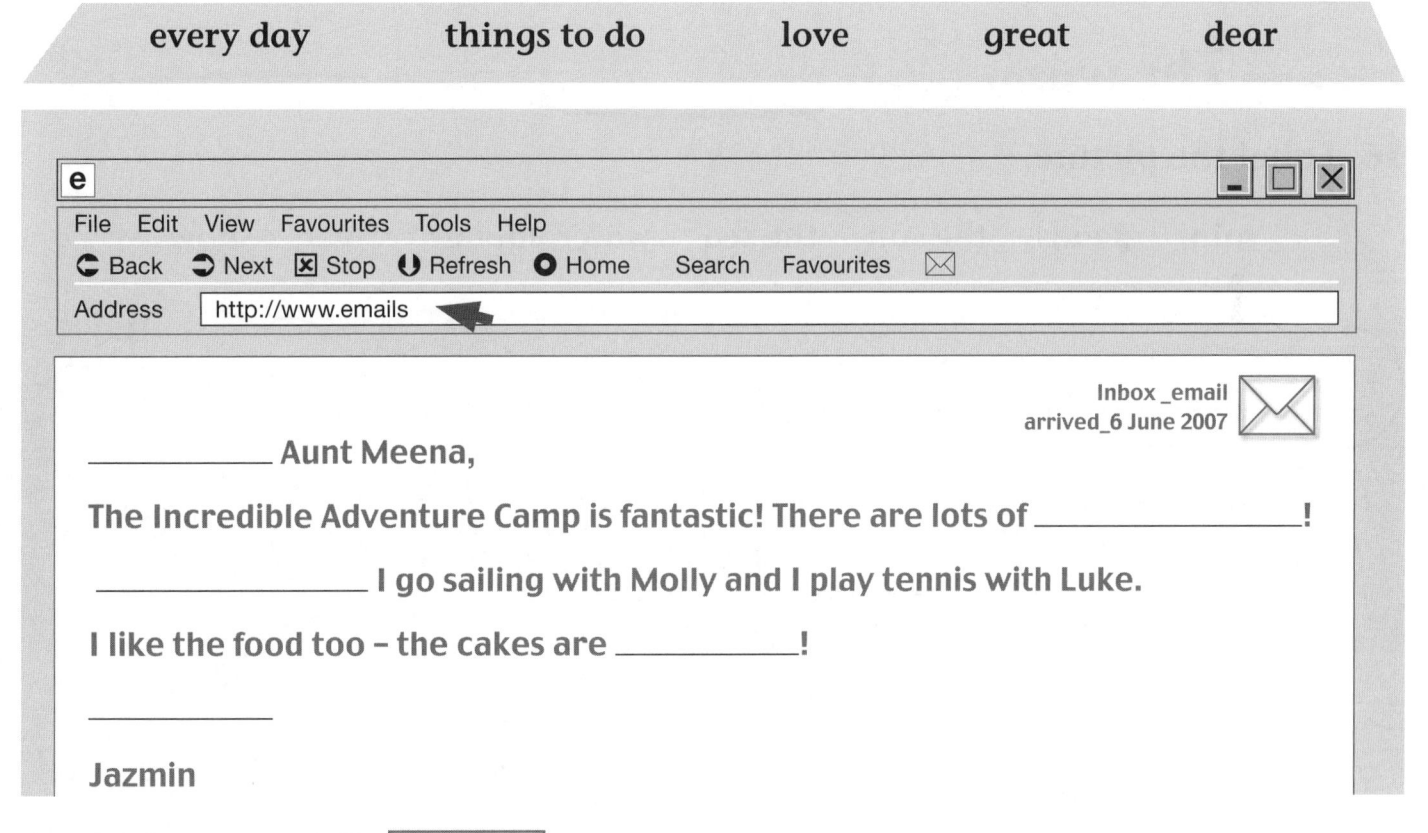

| every day | things to do | love | great | dear |

_____ Aunt Meena,

The Incredible Adventure Camp is fantastic! There are lots of _____!

_____ I go sailing with Molly and I play tennis with Luke.

I like the food too – the cakes are _____!

_____

Jazmin

14 Write an email. PMB page 7

15 Number the lines. Then listen and check. 1.7

song

a Come and swim with me!
b Come and swim with me!
c Let's go swimming, — 1
d I like swimming – do you like swimming too?
e Let's go swimming,
f Let's go swimming, I want to swim with you.

g Let's go fishing, I want to fish with you.
h Come and fish with me!
i I like fishing – do you like fishing too?
j Let's go fishing,
k Come and fish with me!
l Let's go fishing,

The water cycle

16 Label the picture.

rain   clouds   the sun   the sea   water vapour   river   snow

The weather

17 Write the words.

> It's sunny.   It's cloudy.   It's windy.   It's raining.
> It's snowing.   It's foggy.   It's stormy.

1  2  3  4

_____   _____   _____   _____

5 **FOG**   6    7

_____   _____   _____

18 Read and write.

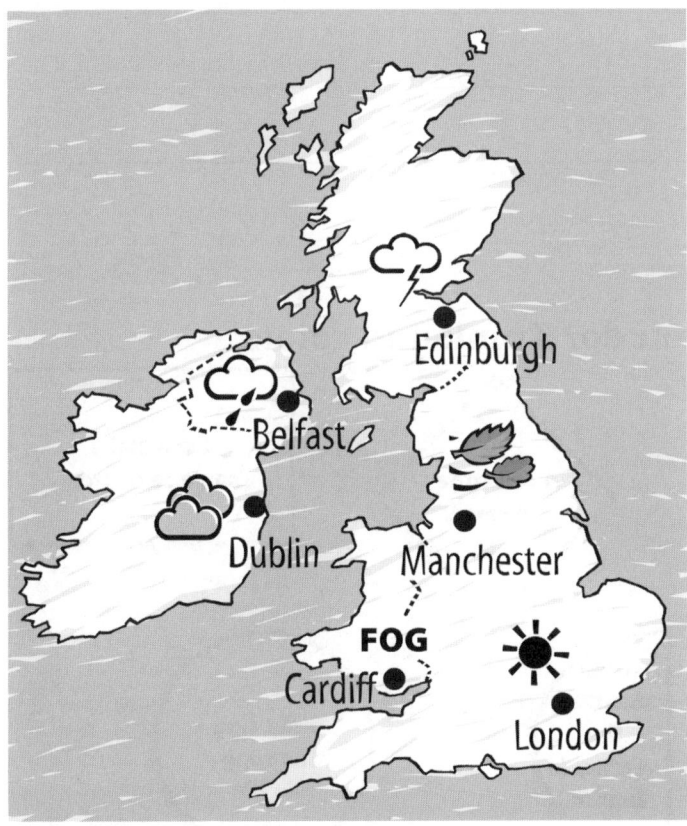

It's _____ in Belfast.

In _____ it's cloudy.

It's _____ in Manchester

and in Cardiff it's _____.

The weather isn't very nice in

Edinburgh. It's _____.

But in _____ it's a beautiful

day and it's _____.

Science   Unit 1   **11**

19 Say. Write the words in the correct box.

20 Find the words.

snow slide swimming swing sleep scooter sticker ~~snake~~ stand skiing

s	p	d	l	j	e	v	c	a	s
c	n	f	a	v	s	q	z	n	t
s	l	a	o	s	w	i	n	g	i
s	t	m	k	g	i	x	i	s	c
n	k	a	t	e	m	r	y	c	k
o	s	i	n	f	m	t	s	o	e
w	j	f	i	d	i	u	l	o	r
m	a	t	k	n	n	h	e	t	k
s	l	i	d	e	g	l	e	e	h
l	p	x	f	d	c	b	p	r	a

snake _____ _____

_____ _____

_____ _____

_____ _____

21 Look at the unit again. What can you do? Think and colour.

- I can remember some words.
- I can read the story.
- I can write an email.
- I can make some sentences.
- I can say the chant.
- I can describe the weather in English.
- I can sing the song.

12 Unit 1   Pronunciation /sk/ /sw/ /sn/ /sl/ and /st/   Review of the unit

Show what you know!

1 Write. Find the letters and find the mystery word.

| cake | run | mouse | ~~fish~~ | pen | sail |
| banana | | kite | ~~climb~~ | | parrot |

The fifth letter is in  and in    cl(i)mb   f(i)sh .

The second letter is in  and in    _____ _____ .

The sixth letter is in  and in    _____ _____ .

The first letter is in  and in    _____ _____ .

The third and fourth letters are in  and in    _____ _____ .

What's the word? ____ ____ ____ _i_ ____

2 Look and read. Write the names.

1 I play tennis and basketball. I go swimming every day. I don't go skateboarding but I go fishing. What's my name? _____

2 I play tennis and I go swimming. I go climbing a lot but I don't go skateboarding. I go sailing a lot. What's my name? _____

3 I go skateboarding. I don't go swimming but I go sailing a lot. I play tennis. What's my name? _____

4 I go skateboarding and swimming a lot. I don't play tennis. I go fishing a lot. What's my name? _____

Art

1 Number the pictures. Then write.

1 pirate 2 astronaut 3 policeman 4 scientist 5 actor
6 pilot 7 doctor 8 artist 9 firefighter

Wears a uniform	Doesn't wear a uniform

2 Listen and draw the route. 🔊 1.15

14 Unit 2 — Jobs — On / in front of / under / behind / next to

3 Look and write.

1 He's in front of the doctor.   _astronaut_
2 She's next to the policeman.   _____
3 She's behind the astronaut.   _____
4 He's next to the door.   _____
5 He's between the astronaut and the pirate.   _____
6 He's behind the firefighter and next to the actor.   _____

4 Make the words.

spelling

1 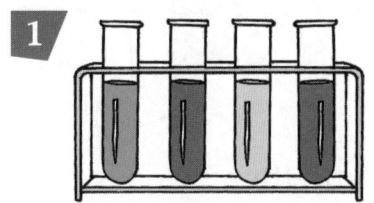 s e t c i i s t n   _____

2  t i r e a p   _____

3  s t a i r t   _____

4 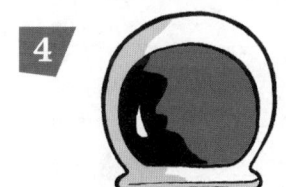 n s a t r u t a o   _____

5 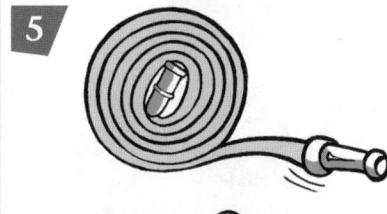 e f i r h t g f i e r   _____

6  m p n l i e a c o   _____

We | get up | at six o'clock | . | She | goes to bed | at eight o'clock | .

5 True or false? Read and tick ✓ or cross ✗.

Jake gets up at seven o'clock. At eight o'clock he has breakfast and then he goes to school at nine o'clock. He has lunch at two o'clock and then he goes home at four o'clock. He goes to bed at 9.30.

6 Write and draw the times.

We   I   They   have dinner at six o'clock   get up at eight o'clock
go rowing at eleven o'clock   have breakfast at nine o'clock

She	always	goes to school	at nine o'clock	.
He	usually	gets up	early	.
He	never	goes to bed	late	.

7 Listen and tick ✓. 1.18

	always	usually	never
Get up at 6 o'clock	✓		
Have breakfast at seven o'clock			
Go to work at eight o'clock			
Have lunch at one o'clock			
Go to bed at ten o'clock			

Read and tick ✓.

> I never get up early. I never have breakfast, I don't like breakfast. I usually go to work at 10 o'clock. I always have lunch at 3 o'clock.

	always	usually	never
Get up early			
Have breakfast			
Go to work at ten o'clock			
Have lunch at three o'clock			

8 Write your daily routine.

_____
_____
_____
_____

◆ *always / usually / never*

9 Listen to the story again. 1.16

10 Write the words in groups.

usually   a pencil   a dancer   a pen   car
a teacher   never   van   a brush   an actor

some paint   an artist   always   bike

11 Choose words and complete the playscript. Act.

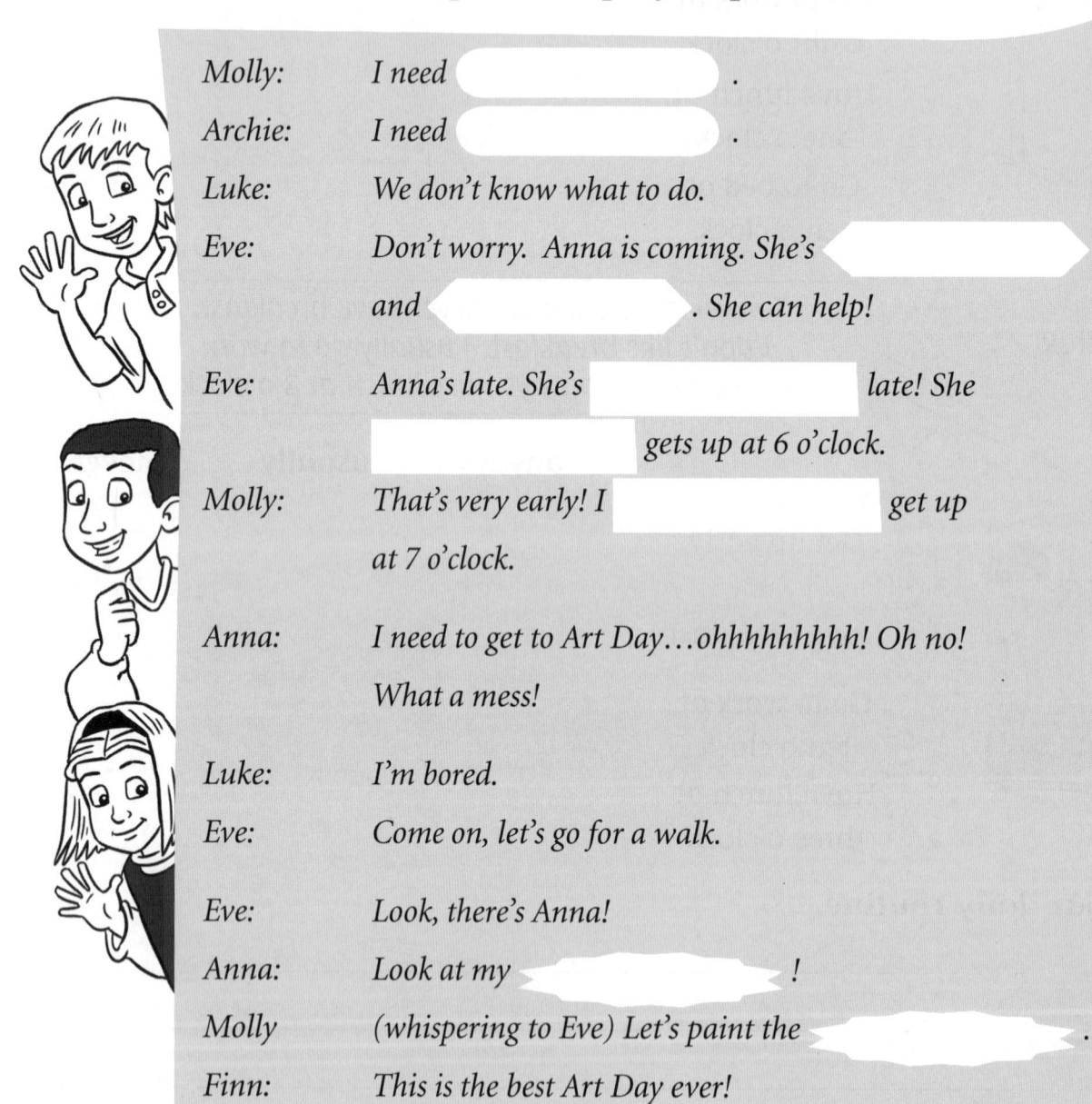

Molly:	I need _____.
Archie:	I need _____.
Luke:	We don't know what to do.
Eve:	Don't worry. Anna is coming. She's _____ and _____. She can help!
Eve:	Anna's late. She's _____ late! She _____ gets up at 6 o'clock.
Molly:	That's very early! I _____ get up at 7 o'clock.
Anna:	I need to get to Art Day…ohhhhhhhh! Oh no! What a mess!
Luke:	I'm bored.
Eve:	Come on, let's go for a walk.
Eve:	Look, there's Anna!
Anna:	Look at my _____!
Molly:	(whispering to Eve) Let's paint the _____.
Finn:	This is the best Art Day ever!

12 Read and complete the notes.

Notices

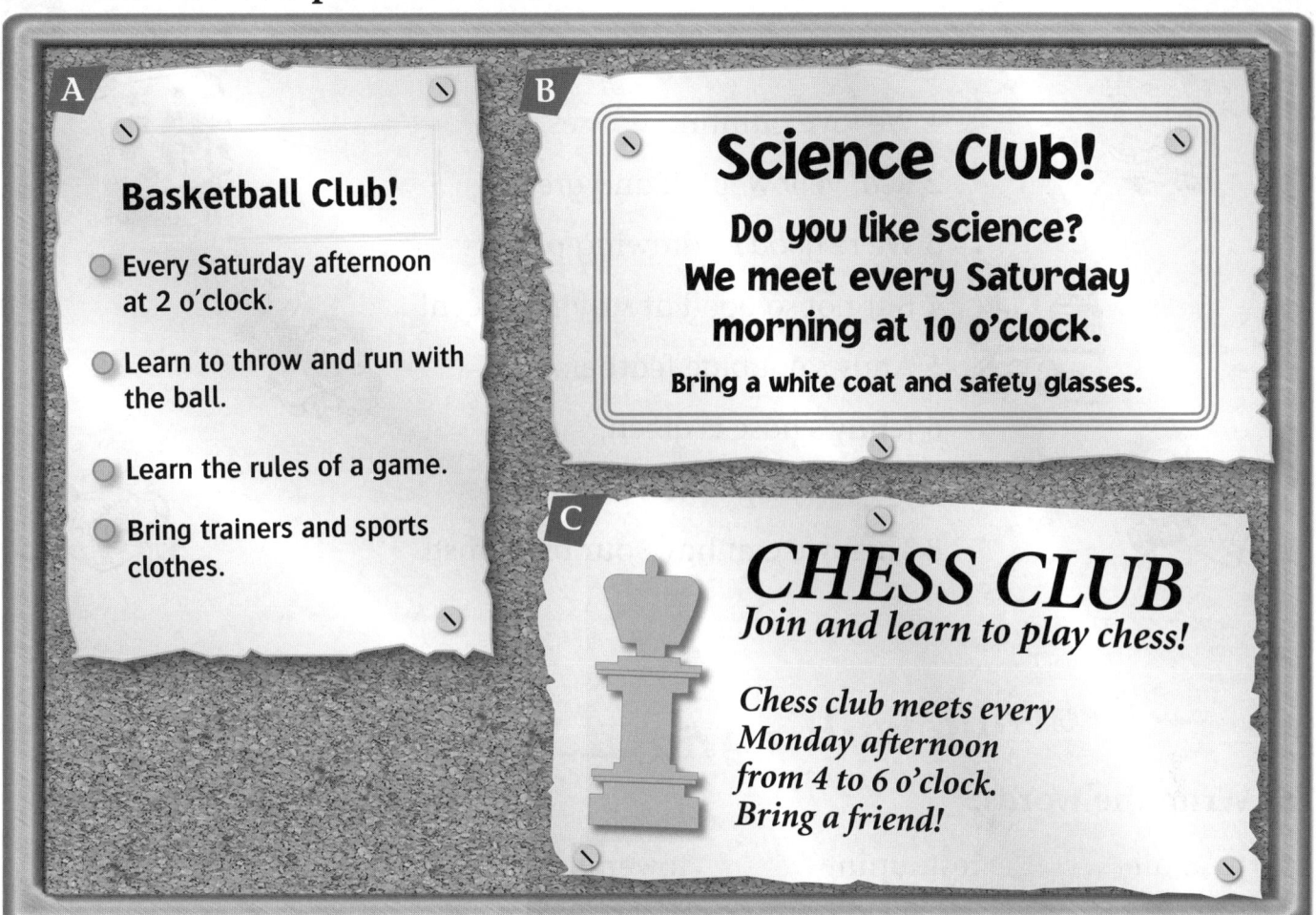

What?	Basketball Club	_____	_____
What day?	_____	_____	_____
What time?	_____	_____	_____
What should you bring?	_____	_____	_____

13 Write 2 notices. PMB page 12

14 Read and correct. Then listen and check. 1.19

1 We love painting ~~houses~~, _pictures_
2 Red, yellow, pink and green,
3 We're good at drawing pictures,
4 But not so good at staying green!
5 Andy's got blue feathers,
6 Jenny's nose is green,
7 Let's tidy up and wash our feet,
8 Then we can have our breakfast!

Drawing with a grid

15 Write the words.

| stairs | restaurant | tower | lift | 533m high |

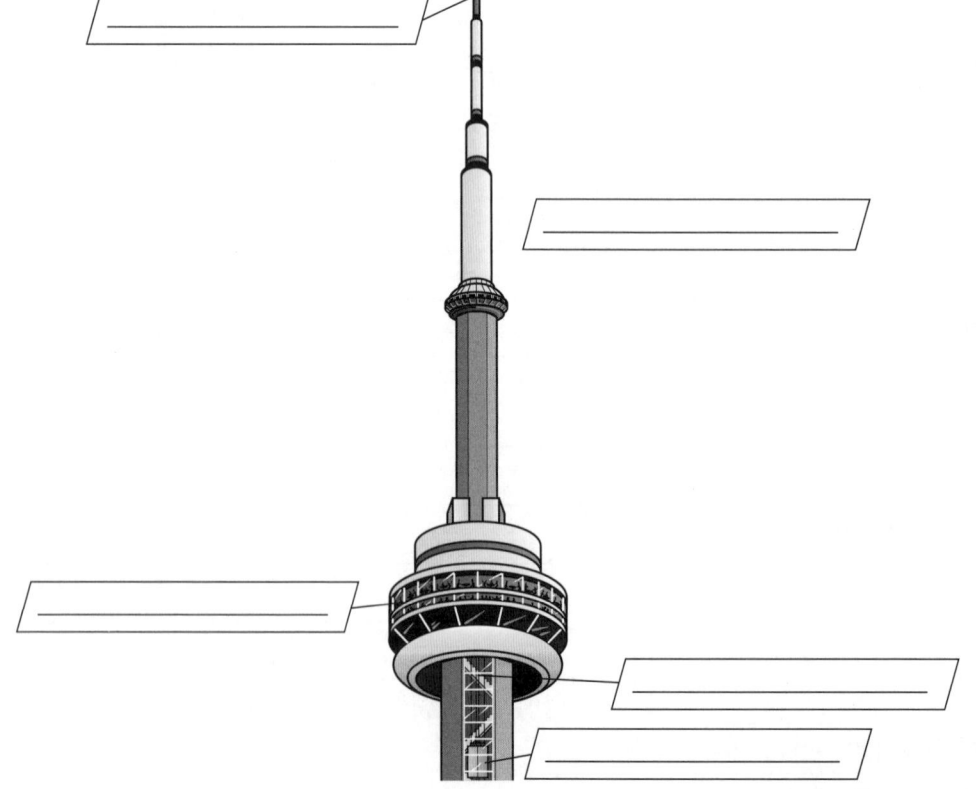

Drawing with a grid

16 Look and write.

> It's in Italy.   It's 98m high.   It's in Poland.   It's 329m high.
> It's 230m high.   It's in France.   It's 55m high.   It's in England.

_____   _____   _____   _____
_____   _____   _____   _____

17 Copy the grid. Then draw.

18 Say. Circle the sound.

doct(or)   pilot   /ə/   actor   singer

dancer   postman   pirate   policeman

sailor   soldier

19 Write the words. What's the secret word?

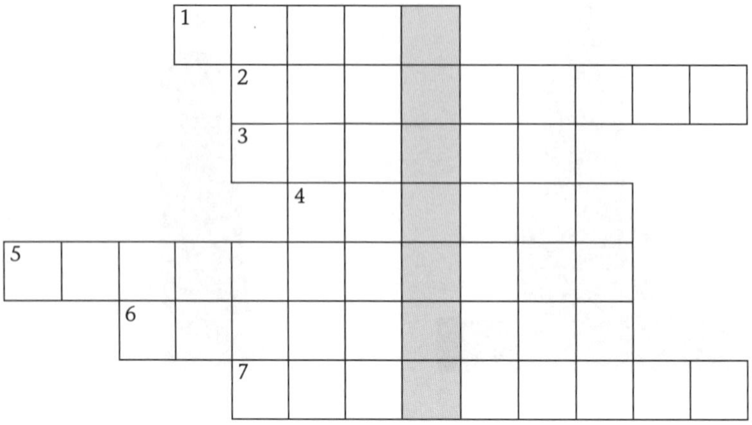

The secret word is _____

20 Look at the unit again. What can you do? Think and colour.

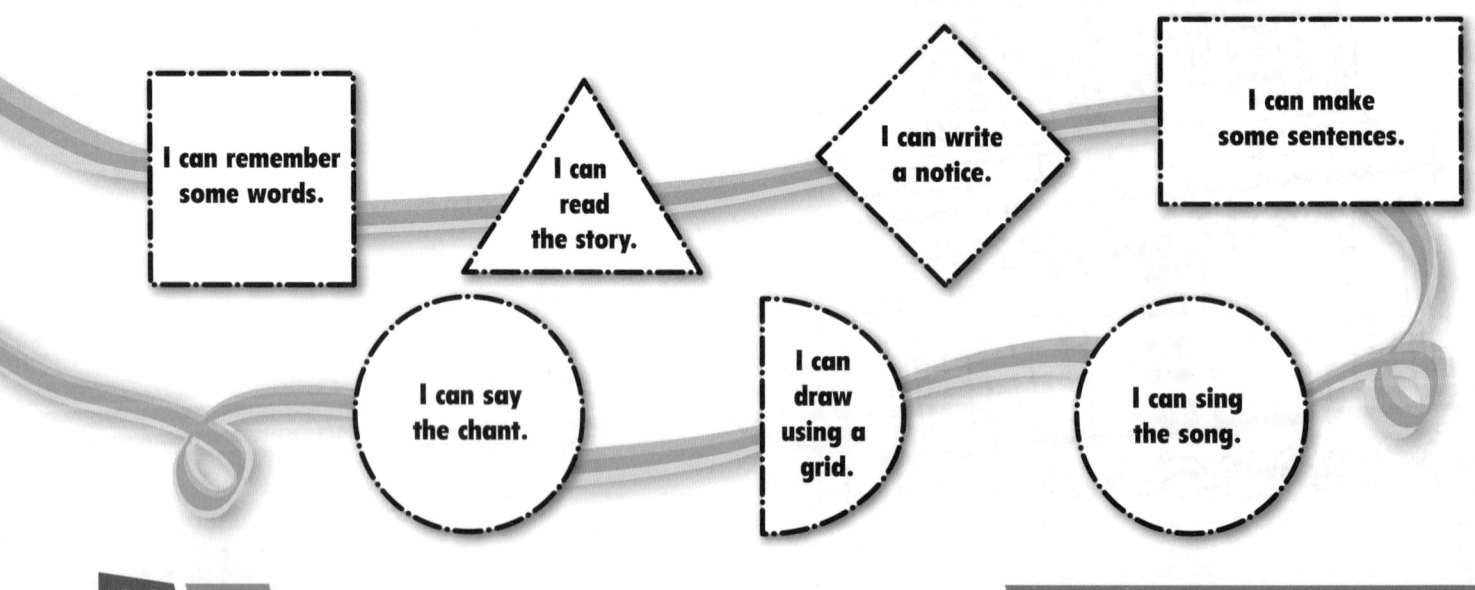

I can remember some words.

I can read the story.

I can write a notice.

I can make some sentences.

I can say the chant.

I can draw using a grid.

I can sing the song.

Show what you know! 2

1 Find the words. Write sentences.

1 ehdnbi   behind
Coco's behind the tree.

2 ni rofnt fo   _____

3 nxte ot   _____

4 beeewnt   _____

2 Write the jobs.

| firefighter | policeman | footballer | teacher |
| dancer | actor | doctor | scientist | pilot | astronaut |

| I wear a uniform. | I play a sport. | I work at a school. | I work in a theatre. | I wear a white coat. | I fly in a machine. |

3 Make sentences.

1 get up / I / early / never
_____

2 always / I / for breakfast / have / toast
_____

3 I / on Saturday morning / go swimming / usually
_____

4 to school / my teacher / on the bus / always / goes
_____

Revision   23

3 Health

1 Number the pictures. Then write.

1 dizzy 2 an earache 3 a headache 4 a cold
5 a sore throat 6 a toothache 7 sick 8 a stomach ache

I feel	I've got
_____	_____
_____	_____
_____	_____
_____	_____
_____	_____

2 Listen and tick ✓. 1.27

	Tommy	Jess	George
sick			
a cough			
a sore throat	✓		
a headache			
an earache			
a stomach ache			

3 Read and write.

Dear Mrs Murphy,
I'm afraid that Tommy can't come to school today. He isn't well. He's got _____, _____ and _____

Best wishes,
Mrs Smith
(Tommy's mum)

Dear Mrs Murphy,
I'm afraid that Jess can't come to school today. She isn't well.
She's _____
_____
_____

Best wishes,
Mrs Salter (Jess's mum)

Dear Mr Owen,
I'm afraid that George can't come to the match today. He isn't well.
He's _____
_____
_____

Best wishes,
Mr Wood
(George's dad)

4 Complete the words. Find the secret word.

spelling

1 h □ a d a __ h __
2 __ o o __ h □ c __ __
3 s __ □ e   __ __ r o __ t
4 __ __ o m □ c h   __ c h __
5 □ __ l d
6 __ o __ g □
7 O h   d □ __ __ !

I've got an _____ .

I've got...   Spelling: Illnesses

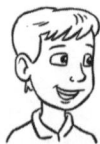

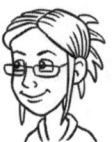

You should	sit still	.	You shouldn't	eat sweets	.

5 What should they do? Read and tick ✓ or cross ✗. Write.

run   watch TV   go to bed   eat sweets   eat a sandwich   drink some water

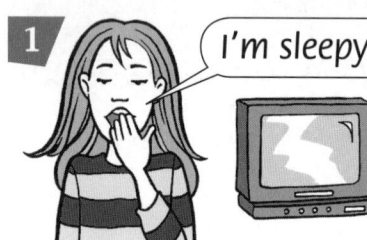

1
I'm sleepy.

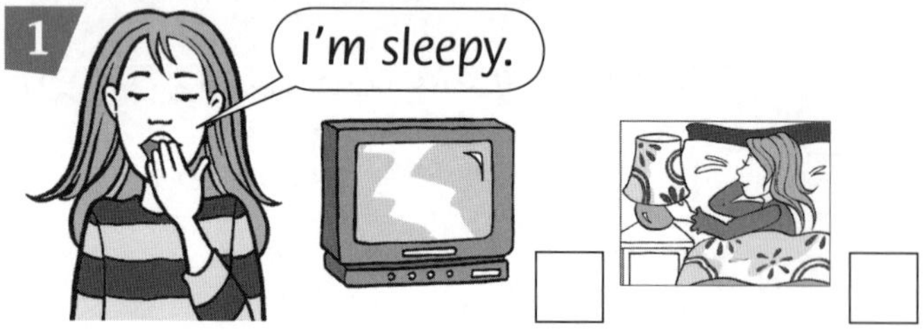

You shouldn't watch TV.
You should go to bed.

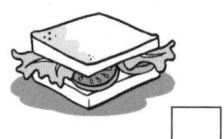

2
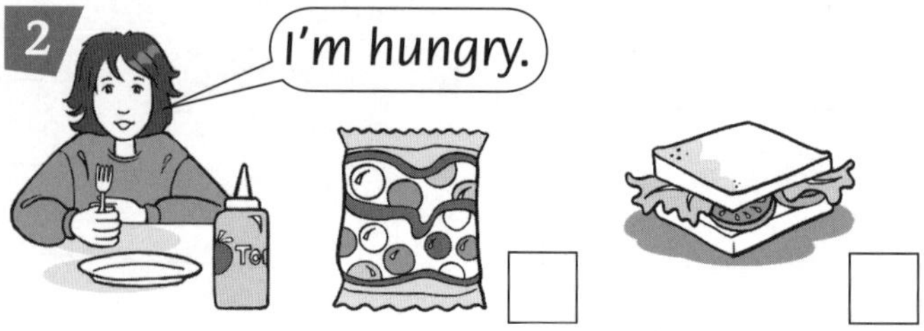
I'm hungry.

____
____

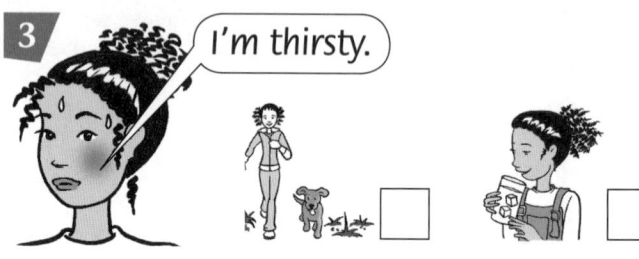

3
I'm thirsty.

____
____

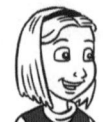

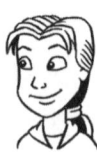

Can you help	me	?	I can help	you	.

6 Listen and number. 1.30

School

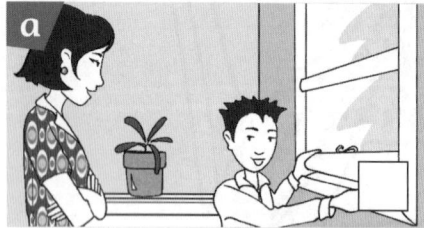

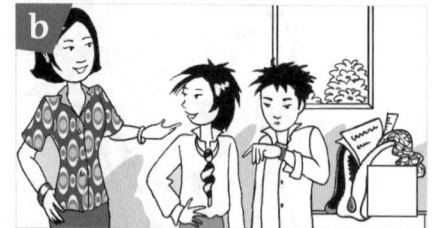

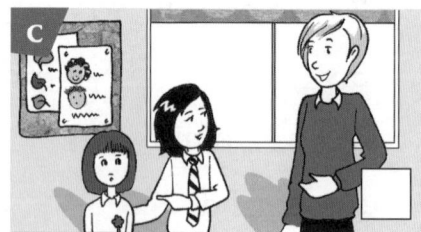

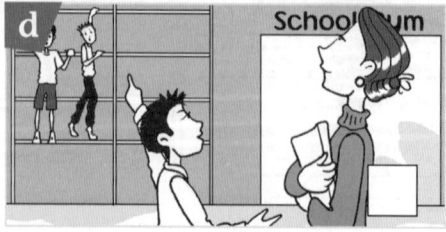

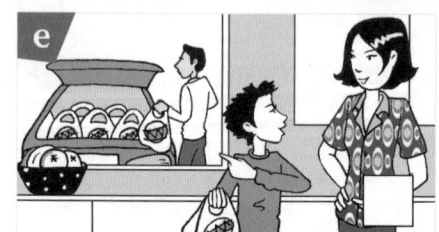

7 Listen again and write the questions. 🔊 1.30

| ~~us~~ | me | them | him | her |

1 Can you help __us__?   4 Can you help _____?
2 Can you help _____?   5 Can you help _____?
3 Can you help _____?

8 Write the questions.

| have a pizza   play basketball   go to the cinema | with us   with them |
| play   play on the computer | with me |

Do you want to have a pizza with me?

9 Listen to the story again. 1.28

10 Write the words in groups.

rest   biscuits   cakes   be quiet
sick   bananas   headache

apples   sit still   dizzy   stomach ache

11 Choose words and complete the playscript. Act.

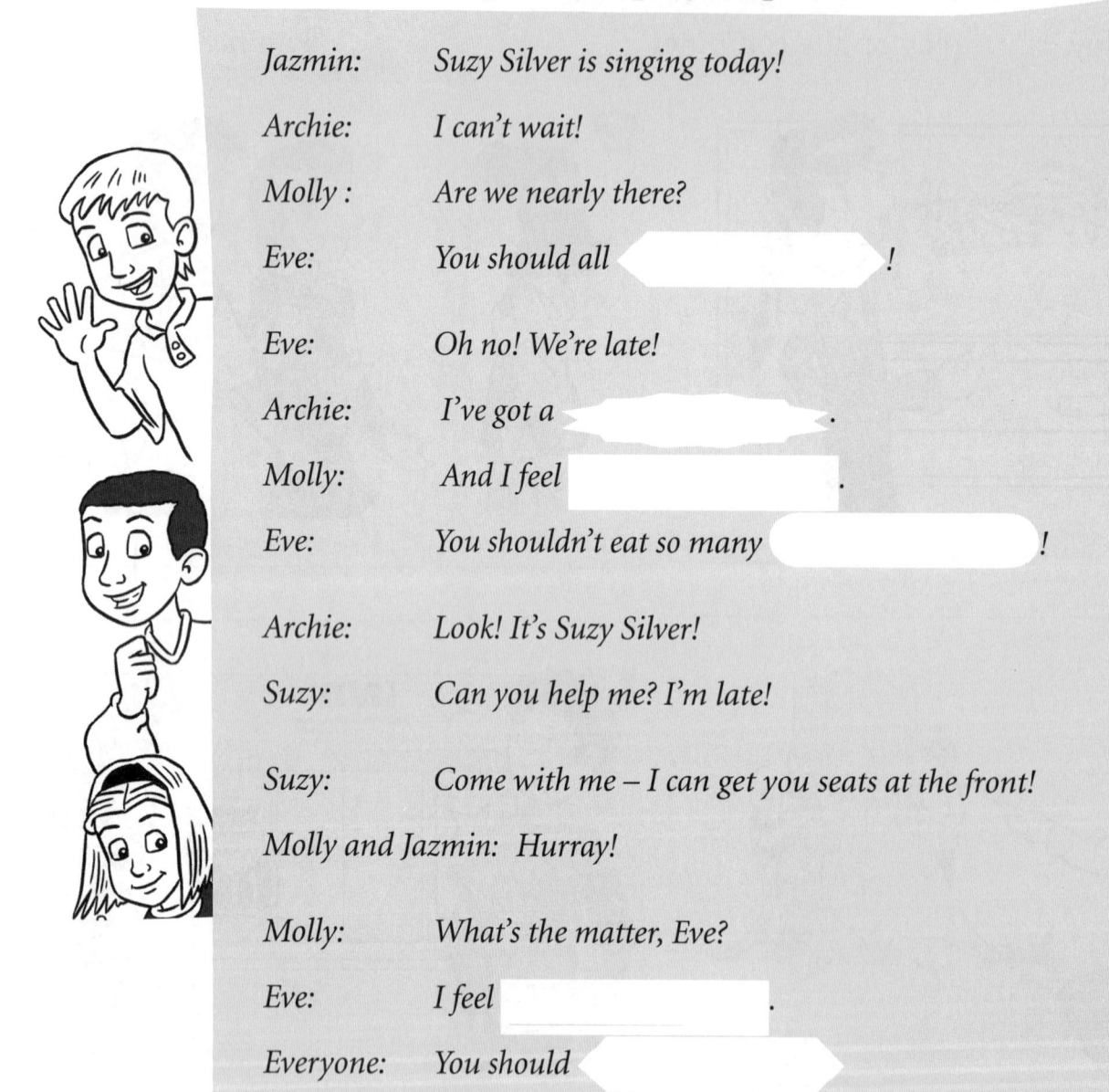

Jazmin: Suzy Silver is singing today!

Archie: I can't wait!

Molly: Are we nearly there?

Eve: You should all _____!

Eve: Oh no! We're late!

Archie: I've got a _____.

Molly: And I feel _____.

Eve: You shouldn't eat so many _____!

Archie: Look! It's Suzy Silver!

Suzy: Can you help me? I'm late!

Suzy: Come with me – I can get you seats at the front!

Molly and Jazmin: Hurray!

Molly: What's the matter, Eve?

Eve: I feel _____.

Everyone: You should _____ and _____, Eve!

12 Read and number the pictures.

LOOKING AFTER YOUR CAT...

1. You should feed it every day.
2. You should give it water every day.
3. You shouldn't give it sweets.
4. You should stroke your cat every day.

13 Read and correct the sentences.

Looking after your teeth.

You ~~shouldn't~~ *should* go to the dentist every six months.

You should clean your teeth after breakfast.

You should eat lots of sweets.

You shouldn't clean your teeth every day.

You should clean them before you go to bed.

14 Make a poster. PMB page 17

15 Read and write. Then listen and check. 🔊 1.31

song

bright   basketball   apples   fruit   swimming   climb   bananas   exercise

1 _____ in the morning,
2 _____ all the time.
3 _____ will give you energy,
4 It helps you run and _____ .
5 _____ in the morning,
6 _____ at night.
7 _____ will make you fit,
8 It keeps you strong and _____ !

Pulse rates

16 Write.

heart   fingers   thumb   wrist   blood

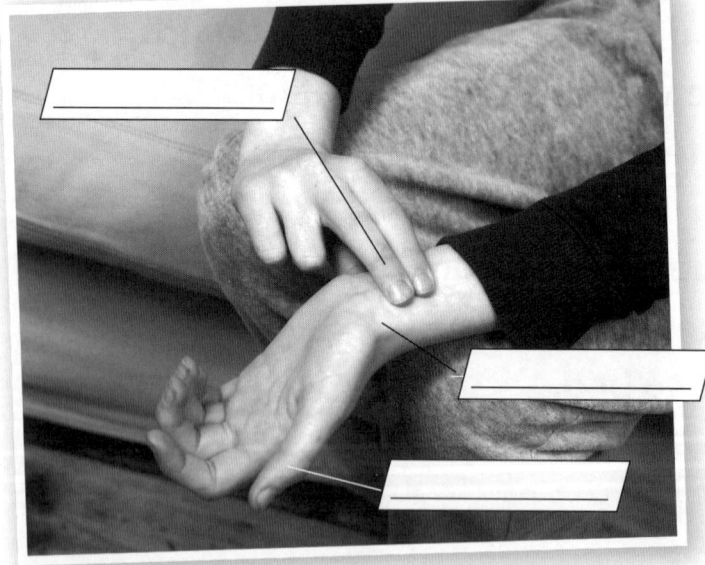
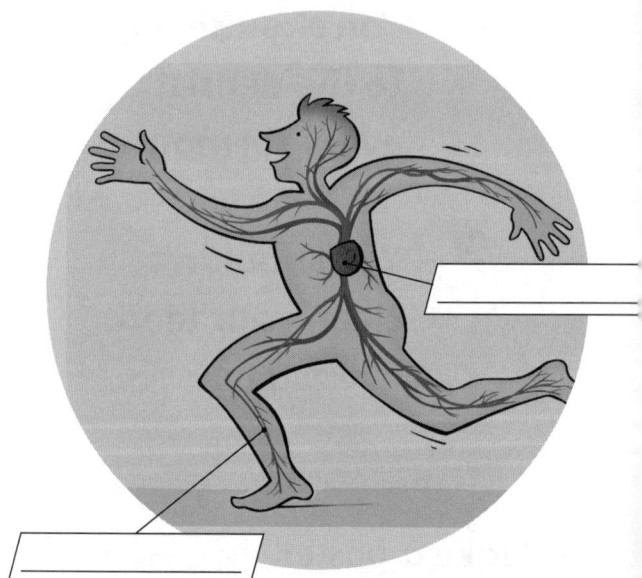

30   Unit 3   Living healthily   ●   Hand and heart

Pulse rates

17 Read and write.

| walking fast | sleeping | running | walking |

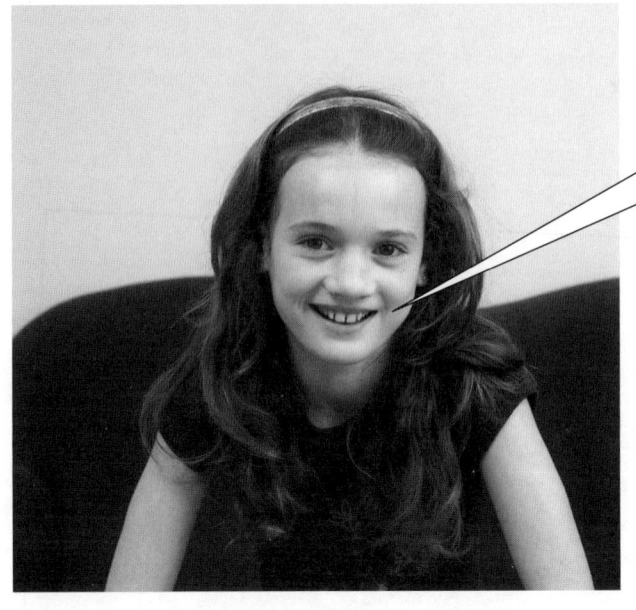

I wake up at seven o'clock. After _____ my pulse rate is 90. Then I get up and have breakfast. At 8.30 I walk to school with my friends. We don't want to be late so we walk quickly. After _____ my pulse rate is 120. Our first lesson is P.E. and we run on the track. After _____ my pulse rate is 140. At four o'clock I go home. I walk and chat with my friends. After _____ my pulse rate is 102.

18 Read and complete.

	swimming	walking	jumping
Pulse rate before	95	95	95
Pulse rate after	130	120	140
Pulse rate after resting for 2 minutes	110	110	110

Before _____ my pulse is _____. After _____ for 1 minute my pulse is _____. After resting for 2 minutes, my pulse is _____.

Before _____ my pulse is _____. After _____ for 1 minute my pulse is _____. After resting for 2 minutes, my pulse is _____.

19 Find the words.

(chicken)chipsfishchoosechocolatecheesechairshoeschildrenkitchenwash

20 Say. Write the words in the correct box.

21 Look at the unit again. What can you do? Think and colour.

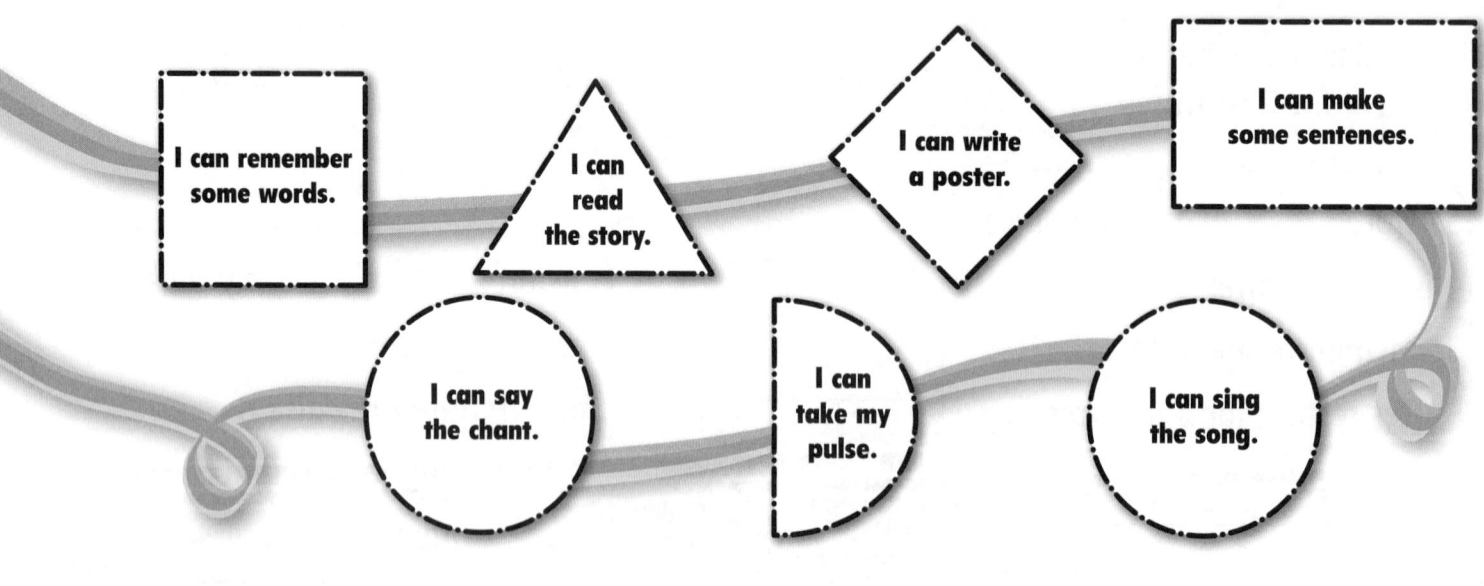

Show what you know!

1 Write the words. What's the mystery word? _____

sore throat   earache   sick   toothache   cold   heart   thumb   wrist

2 Write sentences.

put drinks on the computer   wear a jumper in winter
eat lots of sweets   close the window in winter   work hard at school

1 You should wear a jumper in winter.

2 _____

3 _____

4 _____

5 _____

Revision

4 On the farm

1 Number the pictures. Then write.

| 1 beans | 2 grass | 3 potatoes | 4 onions |
| 5 peppers | 6 cauliflower | 7 weeds | 8 strawberries |

Red	Green

Other colours

2 True or false? Listen and tick ✓ or cross ✗. ◁)) 1.39

34 Unit 4 — Farming — She's watering the tomatoes.

3 Match and write.

| ~~he's eating~~ she's talking he's drinking | grass water ~~strawberries~~ |
| they're watering it's sleeping it's eating | on the phone tomatoes in the sun |

1 <u>He's eating strawberries.</u>   2 _____

3 _____   4 _____

5 _____   6 _____

4 Put the words in the correct box. Write the plurals.

spelling

cherry   pepper   blackberry   tomato

cauliflower   goat

After consonant + y: change to *ies*

strawberry   strawberries

After o: add *es*

potato   potatoes

After consonant: add *s*

onion   onions

He's eating strawberries   Spelling: Plural nouns

There's some | water | . | There isn't any | cheese | .

5 Write questions. Then ask and answer.

1 *There's some milk on this picnic table. There's some cheese and some bread. There isn't any water.*

2 _____

3 _____

4 _____

There are some | tomatoes | . | There aren't any | beans | .

6 Listen and number. 1.42

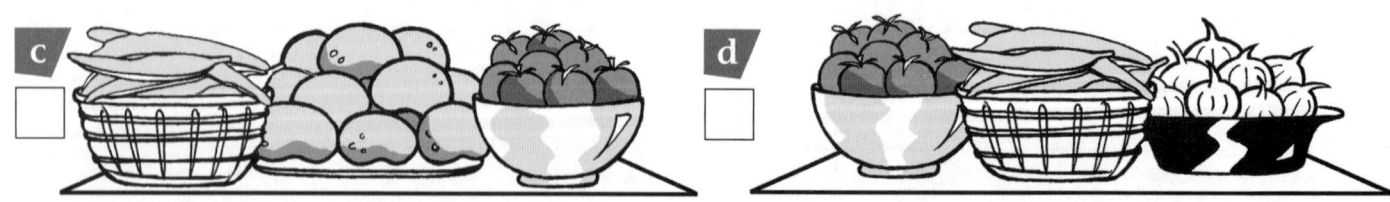

7 Add more words.

milk   potatoes   trees   sugar   bread
tomatoes   water   onions   strawberries   grass

Uncountable
There's some…
There isn't any…

cheese
_____
_____
_____
_____
_____

Countable
There are some…
There aren't any…

peppers
_____
_____
_____
_____
_____

8 Write.

A

1 There are some _____
2 There's some _____
3 There aren't any _____
4 There isn't any _____

B

1 _____
2 _____
3 _____
4 _____

◆ *There's some cheese. There aren't any potatoes.*

Unit 4 | **37**

9 Listen to the story again. 1.40

10 Write the words in groups.

cow   onions   tomatoes   jumper   shoe   strawberries   donkey   peppers

beans

T-shirt

goat

11 Choose words and complete the playscript. Act.

Eve:	OK, Finn, you get water. There's some water over here. Molly and Luke, you pick the _____. Archie, you water the _____. Thanks, kids, you're a great help.
Finn:	Coco! Scat cat!
Archie:	Watch out! Now my _____ is wet. Oh dear!
Molly:	OK. Let's pick the _____ now.
Archie:	And let's water the _____.
Finn:	Oh no! The _____! Look!
Eve:	Have you got the _____ for lunch? Good work, kids. What's the matter?
Archie:	Nothing!
Finn:	Ouch. That hurts!
Archie:	We're sorry, Eve.
Eve:	It's OK – they're weeds!
Finn:	So we are a great help!
Molly:	(to the _____). And so are you!

12 Read and complete.

Notes

for a walk   please   the onions   ~~the windows~~
give some water   the tomatoes   please

1
Eve,
Can you help me with some jobs?

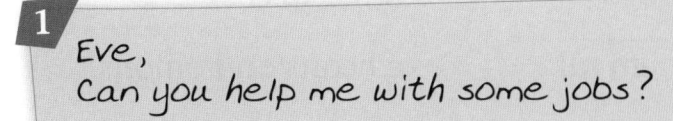

• Please clean ___the windows___ in the kitchen.
• _____ water the onions in the field.

Thanks!
See you later,
Pam

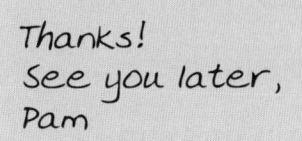

2
Luke,
Can you help me with some jobs?

• Please _____ to the dog.
• Please take the dog _____.
• Please water _____ in the greenhouse.

Thanks!
See you later,
Mum

3
Jazmin,
Can you help me with some jobs?

• _____ clean the kitchen.
• Please pick _____ in the garden and put them in the kitchen cupboard.

Thanks!
See you later,
Mum

13 Write a note. PMB page 22

Notes

Unit 4

14 Match. Then listen and check. 🔊 1.43

1 We plant the — a pepper seeds,
2 We plant the — b the weeds!
3 We plant them all — c beans and onions,
4 But watch out for — d and let them grow,

5 We water them — e they're ready,
6 We need both — f yum, yum, yum!
7 We pick them when — g in summer,
8 Then eat them – — h rain and sun,

How plants grow

15 Write the words.

stem   oxygen   leaf   sap   sunlight   air   ~~carbon dioxide~~   water

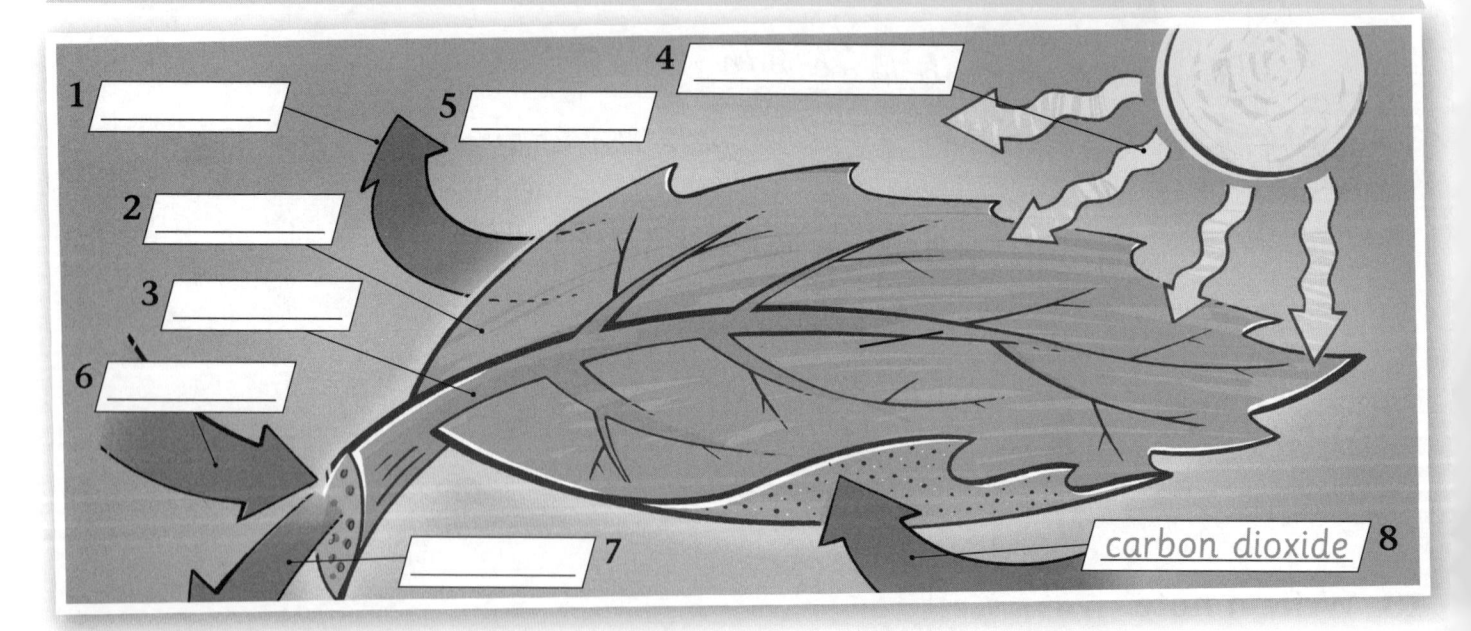

1 _____
2 _____
3 _____
4 _____
5 _____
6 _____
7 _____
8 carbon dioxide

How plants grow

16 Write the words and match the opposites.

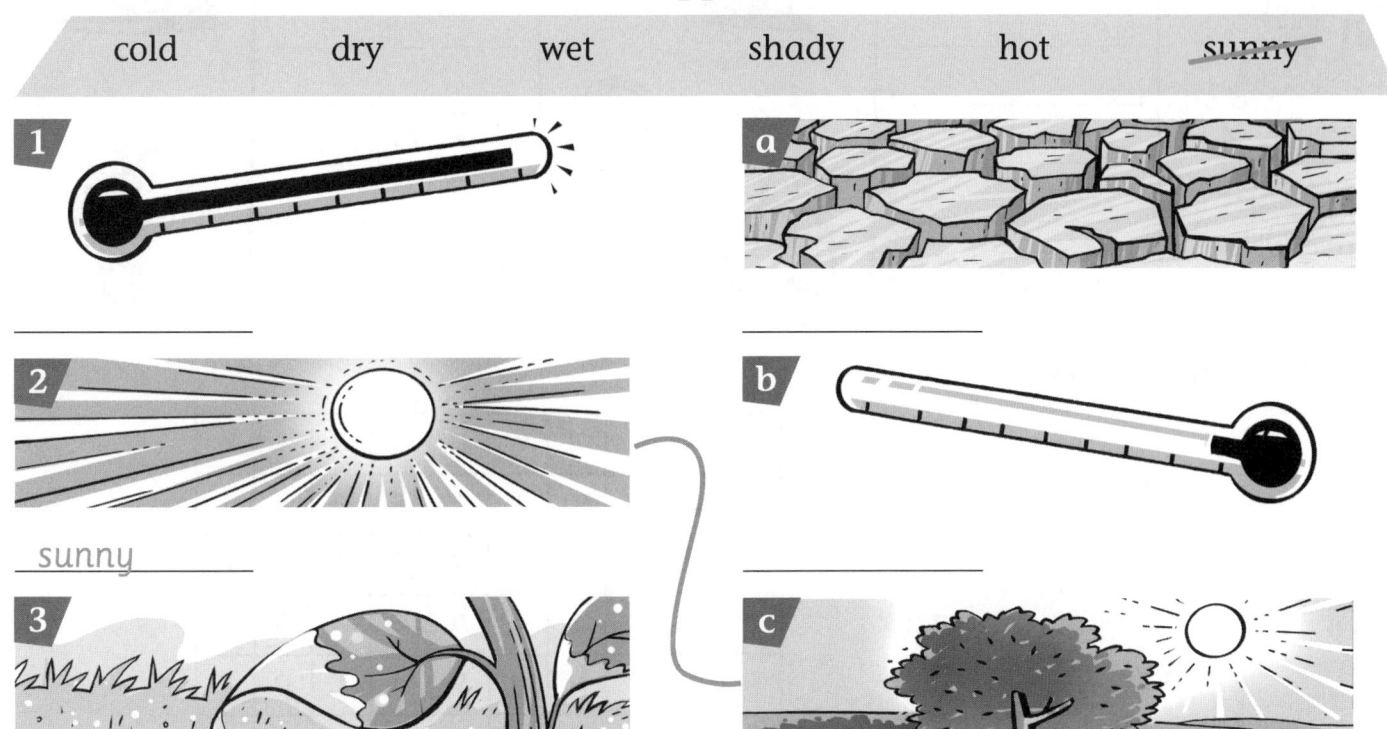

| cold | dry | wet | shady | hot | ~~sunny~~ |

1. _____
2. sunny
3. _____

a. _____
b. _____
c. _____

17 Write.

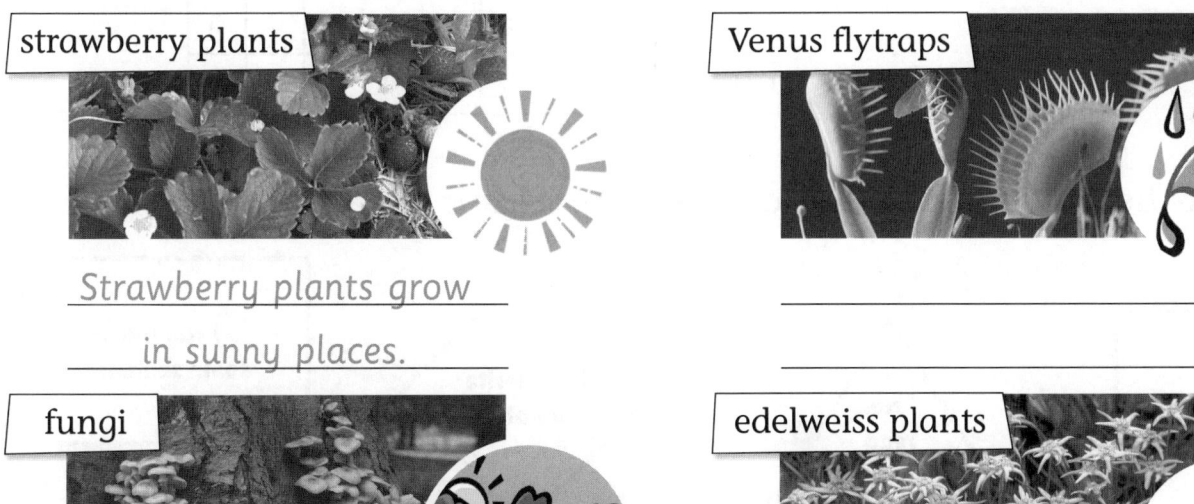

strawberry plants

Strawberry plants grow in sunny places.

Venus flytraps

_____

fungi

_____

edelweiss plants

_____

Science   Unit 4   41

18 Say. Write the words in the correct box.

/əʊ/

goat
_____
_____
_____

/æ/

cat
_____
_____
_____

19 Find the words.

hat   boat   van
~~goat~~   rat
throat   coat
cat   float   bat

r	k	i	z	w	g	o	a	t	w
f	a	h	m	r	f	k	g	x	i
l	d	c	x	a	v	g	m	o	e
o	a	g	r	t	h	c	a	t	j
a	f	e	h	o	y	e	j	p	v
t	a	s	a	f	b	n	u	j	n
d	v	g	t	u	y	a	d	x	c
e	t	h	r	o	a	t	t	v	o
s	j	e	q	l	k	f	y	a	a
b	o	a	t	z	y	e	j	n	t

20 Look at the unit again. What can you do? Think and colour.

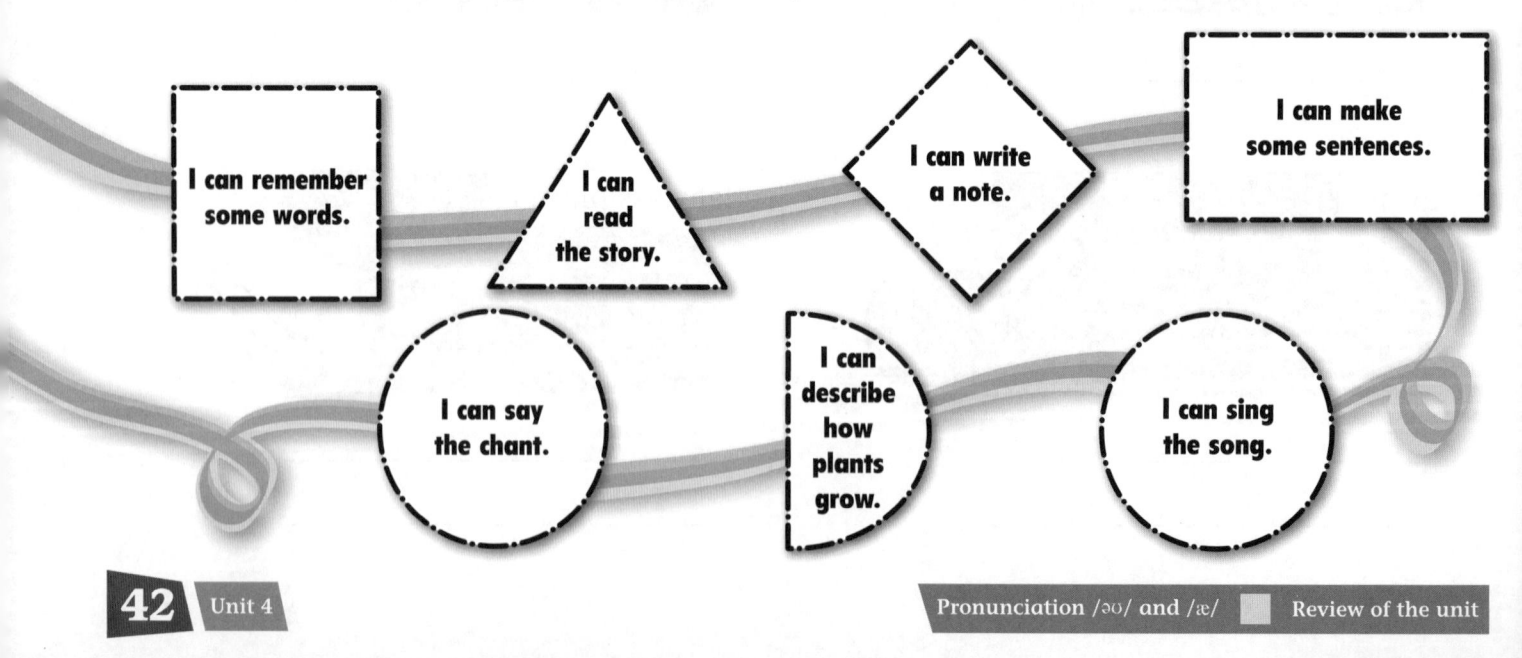

- I can remember some words.
- I can read the story.
- I can write a note.
- I can make some sentences.
- I can say the chant.
- I can describe how plants grow.
- I can sing the song.

42 Unit 4   Pronunciation /əʊ/ and /æ/   Review of the unit

Show what you know!

1 Write. Find the mystery word.

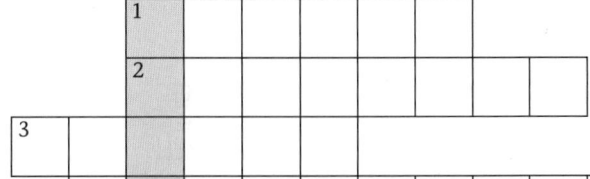

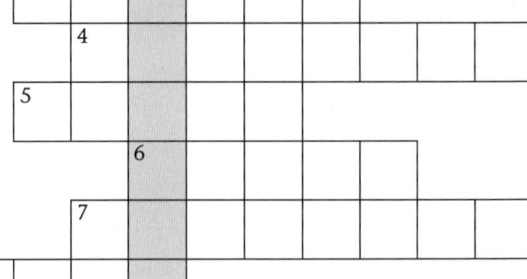

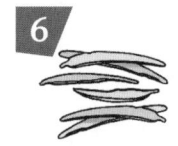

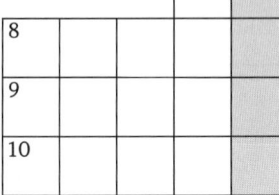

The mystery word is _____

2 Read and number.

1. In my fridge there's some milk and there's some orange juice. There aren't any tomatoes but there are some peppers. There are some onions but there isn't any cheese.

2. In my fridge there's some orange juice and there's some milk. There aren't any peppers but there are some tomatoes. There's some cheese but there aren't any onions.

3. In my fridge there's some milk and there's some cheese. There aren't any tomatoes but there are some peppers and some orange juice. There aren't any onions.

Revision

5 Animal life

1 Number the pictures. Then write.

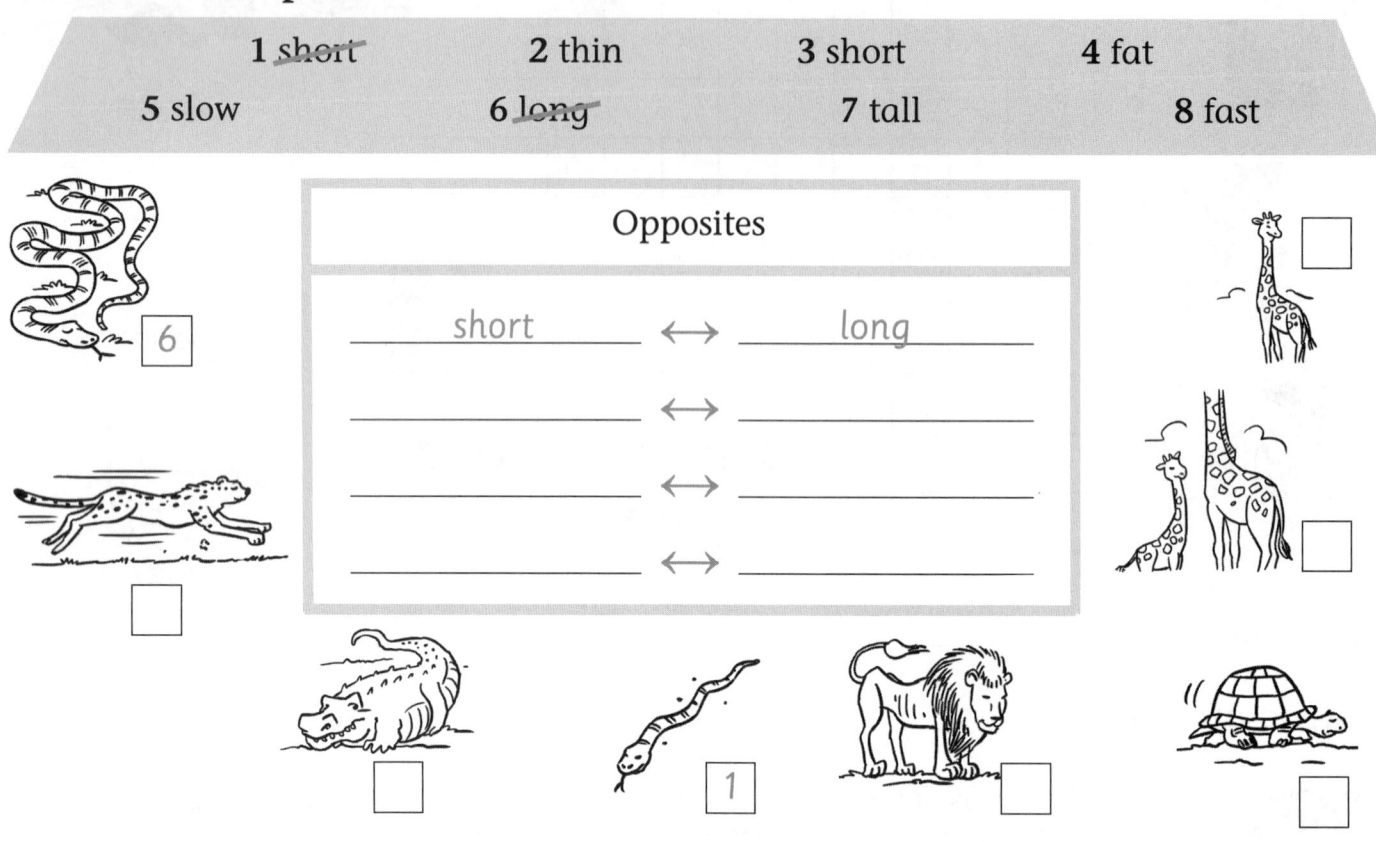

1 short   2 thin   3 short   4 fat
5 slow   6 long   7 tall   8 fast

Opposites		
short	↔	long
_____	↔	_____
_____	↔	_____
_____	↔	_____

2 Listen and number. 2.3

a   b   c   d

44 Unit 5   Adjectives of appearance   Is it ...? It's a ...

3 Write.

strong   thin   fast   small   hungry   fat   slow   big

1 _It's a hungry crocodile and a strong snake._
2 _____
3 _____
4 _____

4 Make the words. Then find the words.

spelling

1 storng   _strong_
2 slwo   _____
3 fta   _____
4 tihn   _____
5 fsta   _____
6 shrot   _____
7 lgno   _____
8 hguynr   _____
9 tlal   _____

b	q	a	p	v	s	t	w	n	c
x	s	h	o	r	t	d	k	e	j
f	d	h	y	e	r	f	i	f	l
a	r	b	w	z	o	g	a	q	v
t	m	u	y	s	n	b	g	s	m
p	t	c	r	x	g	i	h	l	t
o	z	h	u	n	g	r	y	o	c
k	b	c	i	l	m	n	p	w	x
z	r	t	d	n	w	t	a	l	l
h	l	o	n	g	i	e	j	k	s

♦ It's a hungry crocodile.   ■ Spelling: Adjectives of appearance   Unit 5 **45**

Billy's | faster | than Coco | . | Luke's | stronger | than Molly | .

5 Look and write.

1

Luke's faster
than Finn.

2

3

4

Now write 3 sentences about you.

1 _____
2 _____
3 _____

6 Write the words in the correct box.

sadder　　slower　　fatter　　thinner　　shorter
hungrier　　hotter　　colder　　thirstier　　smaller

+ er	+ double letter + er	y i + er

Luke is faster than Finn.

Billy's | the biggest | . | Coco's | the best | .

7 Listen and circle. 🔊 2.6

1 (Jazmin's) / Luke's / Finn's the tallest.

2 Henry's / Billy's / Coco's the fattest.

3 Archie's / Finn's / Molly's the happiest.

4 Eve's / Luke's / Jazmin's the strongest.

5 Jazmin / Luke / Molly is the fastest.

8 Write sentences.

hot   tall   fast   long

1 Matt's taller than Josh, but Sophie's the tallest.

2 _____

3 The Mississippi = 6,270 km
The Nile = 6,690
The Amazon 6,452 km

_____

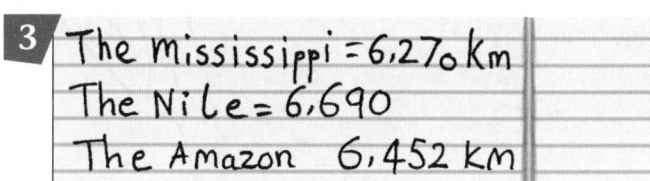

4 The weather around the world today
Manchester 22°C
Mexico City 37°C
Munich 28°C

_____

♦ Luke's taller than Finn. Eve's the tallest.

Unit 5 | 47

9 Listen to the story again. 2.4

10 Write the words in groups.

strongest   bigger   crisps   smallest
stronger   biggest   smaller   pizza   fastest   cake

faster

best

biscuits

11 Choose words and complete the playscript. Act.

Eve: Look – our _____!

Finn: Look – my _____! Get the mice, Coco!

Eve: We need a _____ cat. This cat's _____ than Coco.

Finn: He's _____ than Coco too. Catch the mice, Billy!

Archie: That's Coco's bed! Poor Coco!

Molly: Coco's _____ but she's nicer.

Finn: Well done, Billy! You're the _____!

Archie: Poor Coco. We should help Coco.

Finn: Look, there's the last mouse!

Archie: (whispers to Coco) Go on, Coco, you can do it.

Coco: Miaoooooooooooooooowwwww????

Finn: I'm sorry, Coco!

Archie and Molly: Coco, you're the _____.

48 Unit 5   Story language

12 Read and complete.

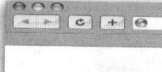

Save the panda!

The giant panda is _____ and white. It lives in _____. It likes _____ places or damp and rainy bamboo forests. It eats 14 _____ of bamboo every day. It is in danger because people are living and working in the forests. There is not enough _____. There are only _____ giant pandas in the world.

Lives: China.
Habitat: cold, wet, bamboo forests
Eats: 14 kilos of bamboo every day
Colour: black and white
Number: 1,600
In danger: People live and work in the forests. There is not enough bamboo.

HELP US TO SAVE THE TIGER!

The tiger has _____ , black and white stripes. It lives in _____ , China and _____. Some tigers like cold, _____ places. Some tigers like hot and _____ places. Tigers eat _____ and deer. They eat once or twice a week. They are in danger because people hunt them. There are only _____ in the world.

Lives: India, China, Russia
Habitat: cold, snowy places or hot, dry places.
Eats: pigs and deer once or twice a week
Colour: orange, black and white stripes
Number: 2,500
In danger: People hunt them.

13 Make a wildlife website. PMB page 27

14 Read and order. Then listen and check. 2.7

a But we're taking all of their water,
b The crocodile lives in the river, [1]
c The monkey lives in the trees,
d And chopping down all of the trees.
e Let's stop wasting all of our water,
f So let's work together to save them,
g Let's save all the animals, please!
h Let's go and plant hundreds of trees,

Bees

15 Write the words.

honey   drone   beehive   queen   comb   worker

1. _____ 
2. _____ 
3. _____ 
4. _____ 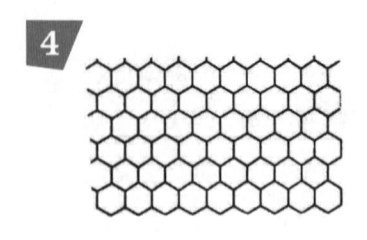
5. _____
6. _____

Bees

16 Match. Find the picture. Write.

1 make — the hive
2 clean — honey
3 make — eggs
4 lay — food
5 collect — the comb

(1 make → the comb; 2 clean → the hive; 3 make → honey; 4 lay → eggs; 5 collect → food)

_____ | make the comb

_____ | _____ | _____

17 Complete the sentences.

lays eggs   very big eyes   queen   work   clean
flowers   honey   the queen

1 The _____ is the biggest bee in the colony.

2 The queen is the only bee that _____.

3 Workers give food to _____.

4 Workers _____ the hive.

5 Workers collect the food from _____.

6 Workers make _____.

7 Drones have _____.

8 Drones don't _____.

Science   Unit 5

18 Look and say. Then write the words. What's the secret word?

faster

The secret word is _____

19 Look at the unit again. What can you do? Think and colour.

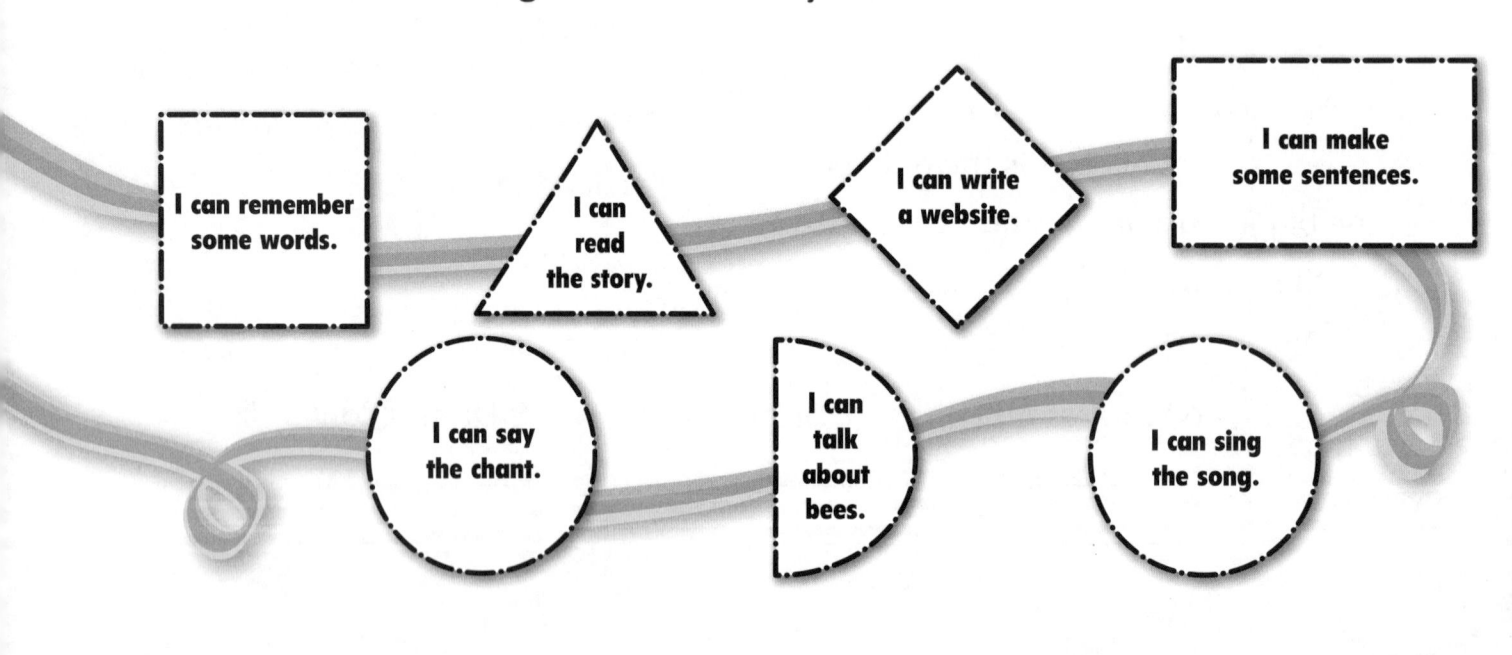

I can remember some words.

I can read the story.

I can write a website.

I can make some sentences.

I can say the chant.

I can talk about bees.

I can sing the song.

52 Unit 5

Pronunciation /ə/   Review of the unit

Show what you know!

1 Write more words.

- Health: I feel sick
- Playing outdoors: go swimming
- On the farm: onions
- Adjectives: fast
- Jobs: pilot

2 Read and write.

1. I'm taller than Molly but I'm shorter than Finn.
   Who am I? _____

2. It's faster than a bee but it's slower than a lion.
   What is it? _____

3. It's younger than Big Ben but it's older than the CN Tower.
   What is it? _____

4. I'm smaller than Billy and I'm thinner than Coco.
   Who am I? _____

Revision

6 Safety

1 Number the pictures. Then write.

| 1 helmet | 2 go right | 3 zebra crossing | 4 stop |
| 5 go left | 6 gloves | 7 traffic lights | |

Road signs	Road	Bike

2 Listen and find. Then number. 2.15

54 Unit 6   Road safety

3 Read and follow the directions.

1 Cross the zebra crossing. Go left. Turn right at the traffic lights and then right again past the car. Where are you? _____

2 Start again. Turn left. Then cross the zebra crossing and walk past the café. Turn right across the zebra crossing and then turn left. Stop before the car. Where are you? _____

3 Start again. Cross the zebra crossing. Go right. Turn left and then right across the zebra crossing. Can you see the traffic lights? Where are you? _____

4 Match. Then listen and repeat. ♪)) 2.16

spelling

1 write

2 right

3 sun

4 son

5 bye

6 buy

7 see

8 sea

◆ *Go right at the traffic lights.* ■ Spelling: Homophones

Unit 6 | 55

You must wear a helmet.
You mustn't run across the road.

5 Write.

wear a helmet   go left   look both ways   stop   go right   wear gloves

1. You must stop.
2. 
3. 
4. 
5. 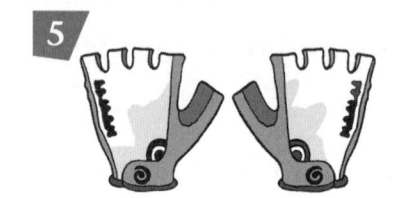
6.

6 Look and write.

eat in the pool   jump in the pool   run   push people into the pool   drink in the pool

1 You mustn't push people into the pool!
2
3
4
5

You must stop. You mustn't run.

| Can I | go and play | ? | Yes, | you can | . | No, | you can't | . |

7 Listen and tick ✓ or cross ✗. 🔊 2.19

8 Match. Write dialogues. Say with a friend.

Dad, can I   go swimming   cross the road
     go out on my bike   watch TV

Yes, but you must   go to bed at 9 o'clock
     listen to the lifeguards
wear a helmet   cross at the zebra crossing

1 Dad, can I go out on my bike?
  Yes, but you must wear a helmet.

2 _____

3 _____

4 _____

◆ *Can I ...? Yes, but you must ...*

Unit 6 | **57**

9 Listen to the story again. 🔊 2.17

10 Write the words in groups.

bushes   let's go   fantastic   gloves   flowers
brilliant   grass   a jacket   water

trees   great   come on   a helmet

11 Choose words and complete the playscript. Act.

Archie:	Look, there's the track
Finn:	_____ . _____ !
Luke:	Stop! Safety first. Listen to me!
Luke:	You must wear _____ .
Jazmin:	Yes, yes, we know.
Archie:	_____ !
Luke:	You mustn't go yet. Listen to me first.
Archie:	_____ !
Luke:	You mustn't ride into the _____ . You must be careful of the _____ and stay on the path.
Others:	Oh all right…
Luke:	And you mustn't ride in the _____ … aaaaaahhhhh!
Others:	He's in the _____ ! Oh no!
Archie:	Look out!
Molly:	Be careful!
Jazmin:	Oh no!
Luke:	OK, OK! You mustn't do that!

12 Read and tick ✓ or cross ✗.

Signs

1 Put your hand up. ☐

2 Shout. ☐

3 Speak quietly. ☐

4 Fight. ☐

5 Listen to the teacher. ☐

6 Throw things. ☐

7 Eat sweets. ☐

13 Write 3 rules.

1 _____

2 _____

3 _____

14 Make a sign for your school or playground. PMB page 32

14 Read and change the words. Then listen and check. 2.20

song

Look ~~up~~ left, look right,
Cross at the rice,
Pink light, red,
Use your bed!

Have a great time on your kite,
Fly fast or slow, as you like,
Wear your tracksuit, use your light,
Enjoy the climb, but hold on tight!

Speed

15 Match and write.

1 100 — c one hundred
2 200 — a eight hundred
3 300 — b five hundred
4 500 — d two hundred
5 800 — e one thousand
6 1,000 — f three hundred

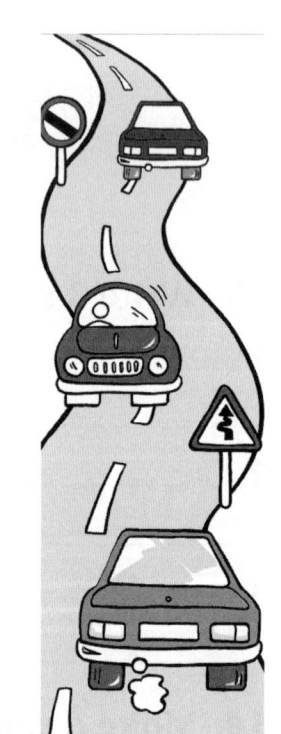

Now write the numbers.

7 400 _____
8 600 _____
9 2,000 _____
10 10,000 _____

60 Unit 6 — Road safety — Numbers 100-1000

Speed

16 Write the numbers.

1 2,451   Two thousand, four hundred and fifty-one.
2 1,156   _____
3 3,790   _____
4 1,380   _____
5 25,560 _____

17 Look at the scales and match.

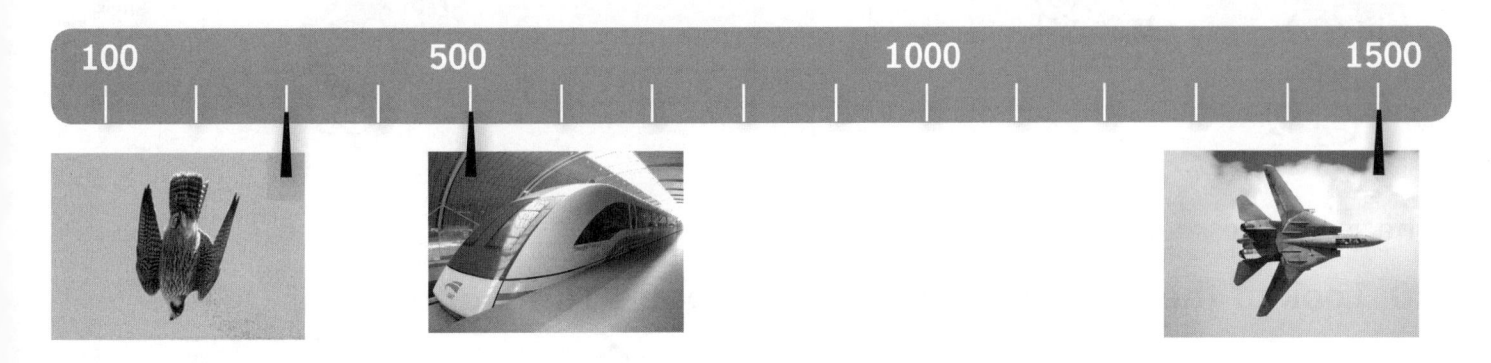

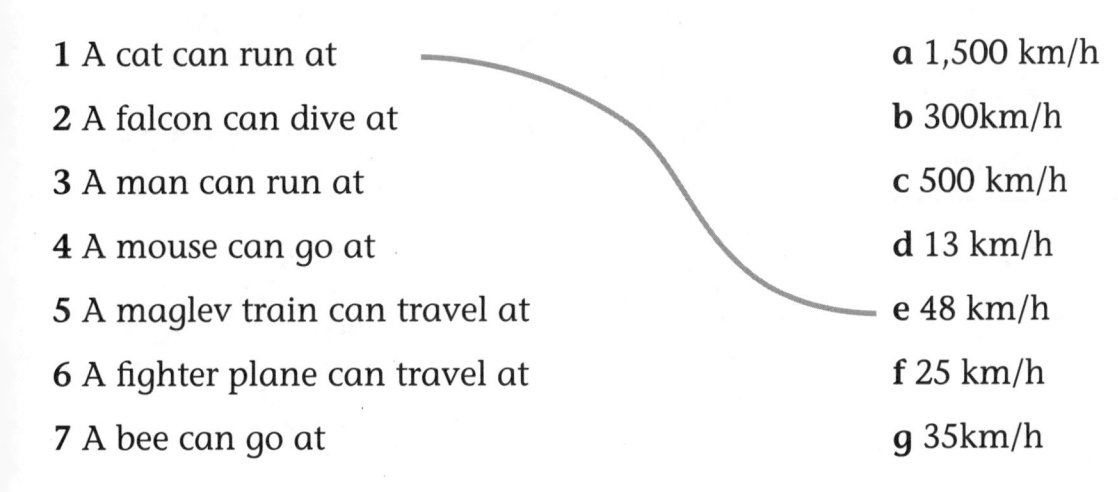

1 A cat can run at   a 1,500 km/h
2 A falcon can dive at   b 300 km/h
3 A man can run at   c 500 km/h
4 A mouse can go at   d 13 km/h
5 A maglev train can travel at   e 48 km/h
6 A fighter plane can travel at   f 25 km/h
7 A bee can go at   g 35 km/h

Maths

Unit 6

18 Say. Write the words in the correct box.

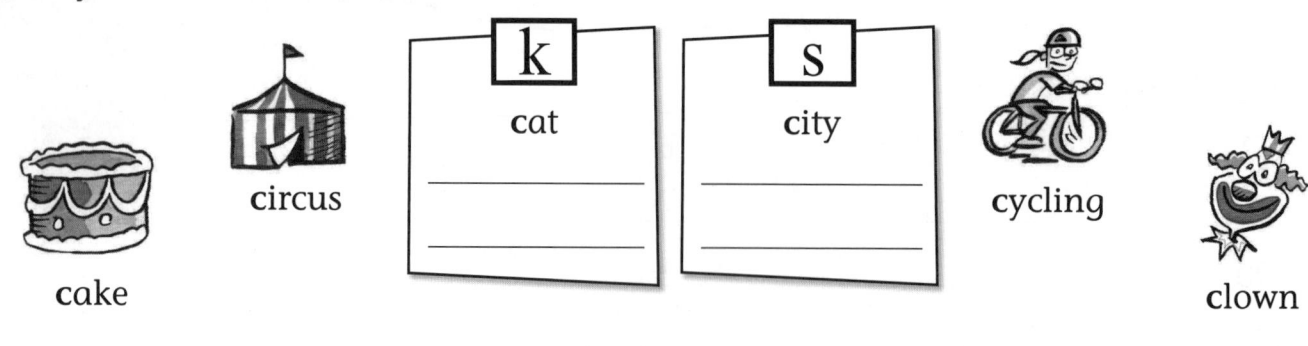

k	s
cat	city

cake   circus   cycling   clown

19 Write the words. What's the secret message?

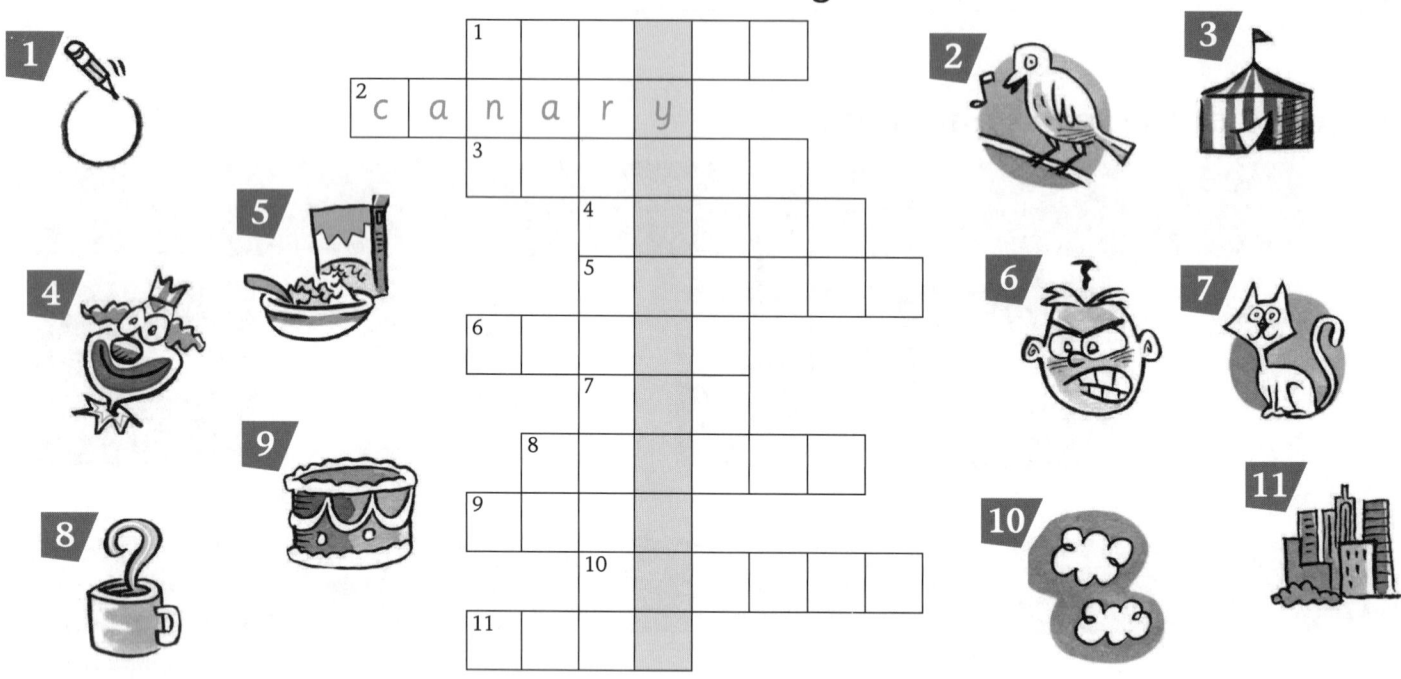

2. c a n a r y

The secret message is _____ _____

20 Look at the unit again. What can you do? Think and colour.

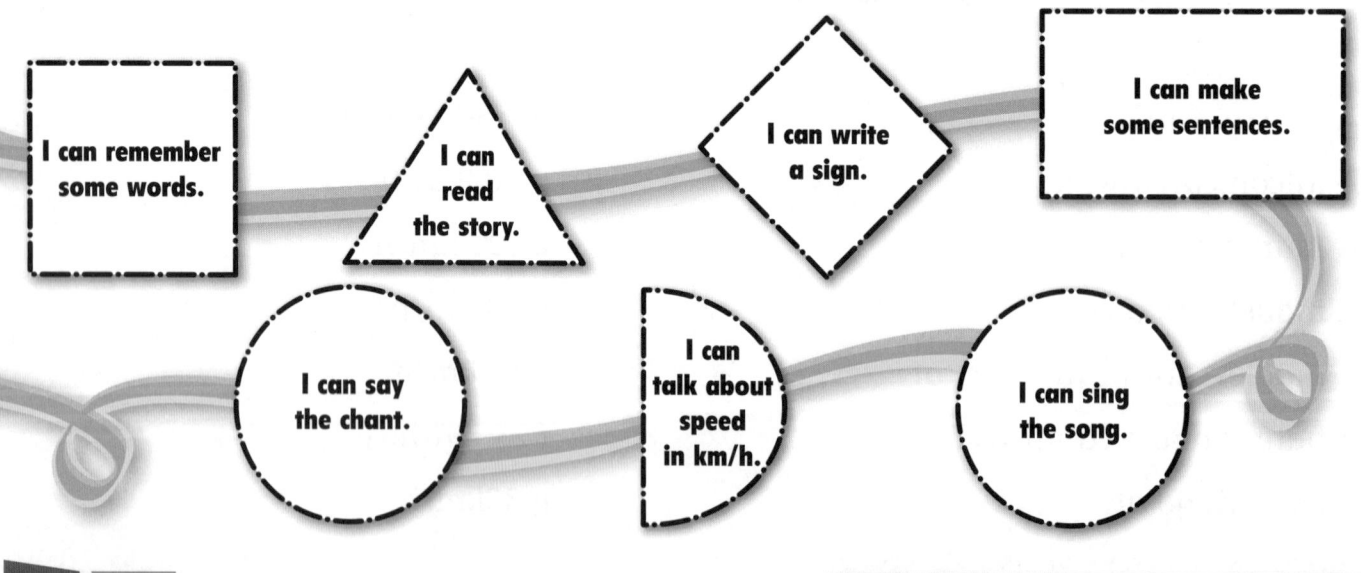

- I can remember some words.
- I can read the story.
- I can write a sign.
- I can make some sentences.
- I can say the chant.
- I can talk about speed in km/h.
- I can sing the song.

62 Unit 6   Pronunciation /k/ and /s/   Review of the unit

Show what you know!

1 Find the words.

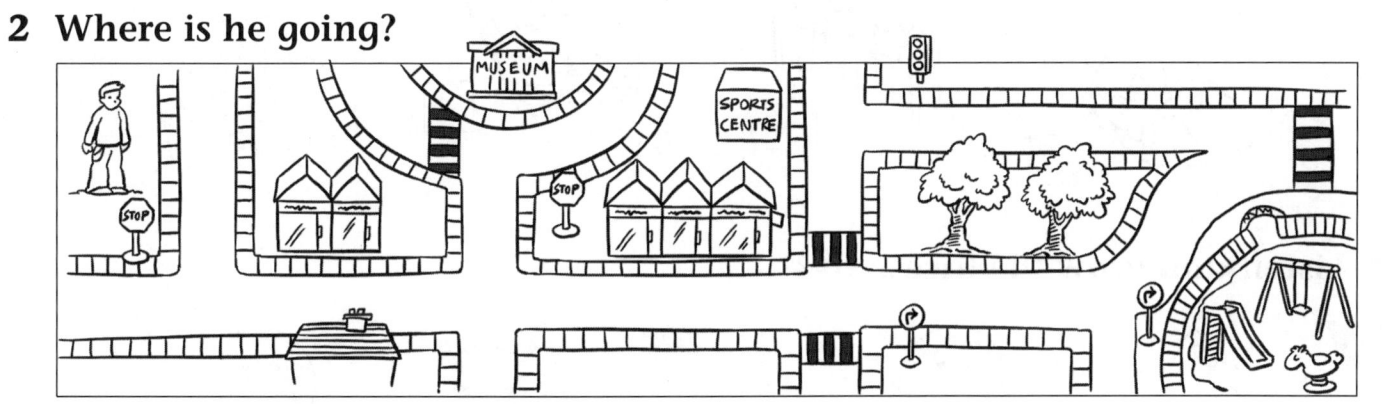

a	e	o	c	o	p	b	u	e	c	m	e	m
i	b	l	p	h	e	l	m	e	t	w	s	d
f	i	t	g	t	e	u	b	q	c	u	t	f
p	k	m	o	f	h	s	t	h	e	k	r	f
b	f	g	b	m	c	p	b	c	o	v	o	m
k	r	e	s	t	a	u	r	a	n	t	n	l
g	b	m	h	l	e	t	c	d	i	l	g	u
m	i	d	b	i	f	r	o	a	d	v	m	e
g	k	f	i	e	c	g	c	e	g	f	o	w
z	e	b	r	a	c	r	o	s	s	i	n	g
t	r	a	f	f	i	c	l	i	g	h	t	s
q	e	b	i	j	s	o	e	m	u	b	u	e
c	o	c	q	o	b	k	s	j	s	o	v	g

2 Where is he going?

1 It's behind three shops, and across the road from the traffic lights.

_____

2 It's next to a turn right sign. There's a zebra crossing on the road behind it.

_____

3 There's a zebra crossing in front of it. There's a stop sign across the road.

_____

Revision

7 At school

1 Number the pictures. Then listen and write. 2.28

| 1 History | 2 Maths | 3 Geography | 4 Art |
| 5 Science | 6 P.E. | 7 Spanish | 8 Music |

•	••	•••
	History	

2 Listen and draw the faces. 2.29

64 Unit 7 — School — I like …. Do you like …?

3 Read and tick ✓ or cross ✗.

This is Grace, Oliver and Martha. Oliver doesn't like Maths.
All the children like P.E. Oliver and one girl like Art. Martha and the boy like Science.
Both girls like Maths. Grace doesn't like Art or Science.

	Art	P.E.	Science	Maths
GRACE				
OLIVER				✗
MARTHA				

4 Write the words. *spelling*

geographyspanishmusicpeartmathshistoryscienceenglish

1 _ r _
2 m _ _ _ _ _
3 _ _ _ e _ c _
4 _ i _ _ _ r _
5 _ u _ _ _
6 P. _ .
7 _ _ _ g _ _ _ _ _
8 _ _ _ l _ s _
9 _ p _ _ _ _ _

He doesn't like Maths.   Spelling: School   Unit 7

| She was | good at Maths | . |
| I was | good at History | . |

5 Write sentences.

Christopher James Secondary School
Year __7__ Annual School report for __Peter Cooper__
Teacher __Mr Alan Black__ Class __7AB 1__

History	8 / 10	Well done, Peter!
Geography	2 / 10	Try harder next time.
Science	7 / 10	
Arts	8 / 10	Excellent work.
Maths	3 / 10	

1 <u>He was good at History.</u>
2 <u>He wasn't good at Geography.</u>
3 _____
4 _____
5 _____

6 Complete the sentences.

| were | were | was | was | was | weren't |

When I _____ at school, it _____ very different! There _____ any computers or calculators. The teachers _____ very strict. The school lunches _____ terrible. But I _____ very happy at Sports Day because I got a medal!

I was good at Art. He wasn't good at Maths.

| Were you | good at Maths | ? | Yes, | I was | . |
| Was she | good at Art | ? | No, | she wasn't | . |

7 Listen and tick ✓ or cross ✗. Then, answer the questions. 🔊 2.32

1 Was Suzy good at Maths?	Yes, she was.
2 Was Suzy good at Music?	_____
3 Was Suzy good at P.E.?	_____
4 Was Suzy good at History?	_____
5 Was Suzy good at Art?	_____

8 Write questions to ask your teacher. Then write the answers.

1 Were you good at _____?
2 _____?
3 _____?
4 _____?
5 _____?

My teacher _____

Were you good at Maths? Yes, I was.

Unit 7 **67**

9 Listen to the story again. 2.30

10 Write the words in groups.

writer   writing   jumping   Book Day
Art Day   Spanish   painting   History   artist

Maths   Sports Day   running   runner

11 Choose words and complete the playscript. Act.

Finn: Come on, Dad. We mustn't be late.
Finn's dad: OK, I'm coming… oh look, there's my old teacher!

Jazmin: Were you good at school?
Finn's dad: I was good at _____. I wasn't very good at _____.

Finn: What about school lunches, Dad?
Finn's dad: Oh, they were terrible.

Finn's dad (to Finn and other children): The teachers were very strict when I was a boy.

Finn: Was there a _____, Dad?
Finn's dad: Yes, there was. I was good at _____.
Finn's dad: I won a medal!
Finn: Wow! That's great, Dad!

Teacher: Hello, young man.
Finn's dad: Hello. I'm telling Finn and Jazmin about my medal at _____.
Teacher: Ah yes, the medal! That was a good day for you.
Teacher: You were the only _____! Everybody was sick.
Finn's dad: It's true! I was good at _____, but I was also very lucky!

12 Read and complete.

Fact files

Hi, I'm Eve. I was at this school 4 years ago, and now Luke and Molly go to this school. Art was my favourite subject but I wasn't very good at it! I was good at Geography and History, but I wasn't very good at Science. I was good at sports. I was best at jumping.

EVE'S FACT FILE

Name: _____
Sports: jumping
Favourite subject: _____
Good at: _____
Not good at: _____
Interesting fact: Luke and Molly go to this school

My name's Archie. I like P.E. the best and I like Geography too. I'm not very good at Science. My favourite sport is running. My dad was at this school too, when he was a boy.

ARCHIE'S FACT FILE

Name: _____
Sports: _____
Favourite subject: _____
Good at: _____
Not good at: _____
Interesting fact: _____

13 Write about you and make notes for your fact file. PMB page 37

Fact files

14 Read and write the missing words. Then listen and check. 2.33

1 Science __is__ at nine o'clock,
2 Geography's _____ ten,
3 Half an hour for break time,
4 _____ then there's class again.

5 I like _____ and History,
6 My favourite _____ is Art,
7 No matter what the _____ ,
8 We study _____ hard!

Ancient Egypt

15 Write the words.

| mummy | pyramid | pharaoh | headdress | god | goddess |

1 __pharaoh__
2 _____ 
3 _____ 
4 _____ 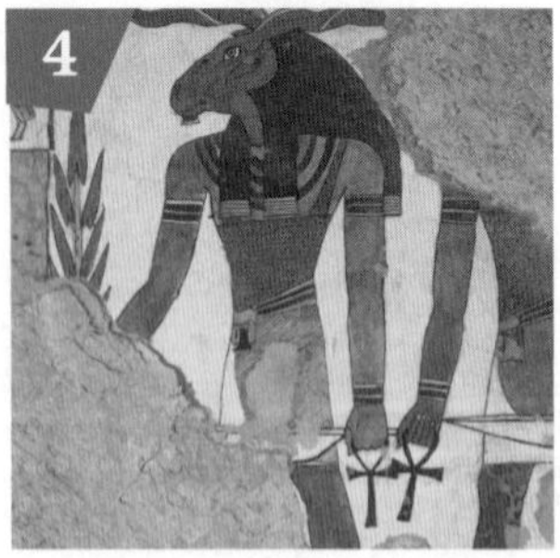
5 _____ 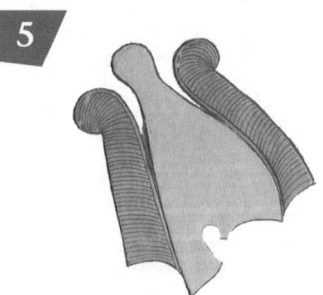
6 _____

Ancient Egypt

16 Write the words.

This is Ra. He was the sun _god_. He _____ the most important god of the ancient Egyptians. He _____ the head of a bird and a _____ with a sun disk.

god   had
headdress
was

This is Tawaret. She was the _____ of women. She had the _____ of a hippo and the _____ of a lion. She had the tail of a _____.

body   head
goddess
crocodile

17 Write about the gods and goddesses.

FACT FILE

Name: _Thoth_
God of: _writing_
Head: _a bird_
This was Thoth. He was the god of _____.
He had _____
_____

FACT FILE

Name: _Ma'at_
God of: _truth_
Headdress: _a feather_
_____
_____
_____

18 Say. Write the words in the correct box.

fish   Friday
thirsty   three
fins   throw
frisbee   Thursday
fingers   thumb

θ

f

19 Find the words and write.

b	c	v	f	i	n	g	e	r	s
f	g	t	n	t	f	e	b	k	t
t	i	k	o	h	r	h	j	n	g
h	e	n	y	u	i	f	i	s	h
u	j	f	s	m	d	k	r	l	t
r	o	r	o	b	a	j	s	o	h
s	g	n	b	w	y	v	d	u	r
d	f	r	i	s	b	e	e	k	e
a	e	t	h	i	r	s	t	y	e
y	t	k	g	t	h	r	o	w	b

fingers

20 Look at the unit again. What can you do? Think and colour.

I can remember some words.

I can read the story.

I can write notes for a fact file.

I can make some sentences.

I can say the chant.

I can talk about the culture of ancient Egypt.

I can sing the song.

Unit 7

Pronunciation /θ/ and /f/   Review of the unit

Show what you know!

1 Write. Find the letters and find the mystery word.

| poster | ruler | dizzy | Art | ~~stop~~ | windy | hat |
| ~~Music~~ | tower | book | fish | yo-yo | cat | bike |

The third letter is in [STOP] and in [music notes]. s(t)op   mu(s)ic

The sixth letter is in [ruler] and in [palette]. _____ _____

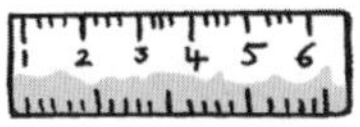

The fourth letter is in [cat] and in [tower]. _____ _____

The seventh letter is in [yo-yo] and in [windy]. _____ _____

The second letter is in [bike] and in [dizzy]. _____ _____

The fifth letter is in [Art poster] and in [book]. _____ _____

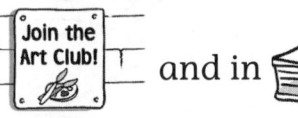

The first letter is in [hat] and in [fish]. _____ _____

What's the word? ___ ___ s ___ ___ ___ ___

2 Make sentences. Match.

1. she / at / Maths / good / was
   _____

2. was / at / Art / good / he
   _____

3. Geography / were / they / good / at
   _____

Revision

8 Underwater life

1 Number the pictures. Then listen and write. 🔊 2.41

1 shell	2 jellyfish	3 shark	4 octopus
5 seahorse	6 sand	7 crab	8 starfish

•	• •	• • •

2 How many can they see? Listen and write. 🔊 2.42

74 Unit 8 — Sea life — *How many fish can you see?*

3 Write the words.

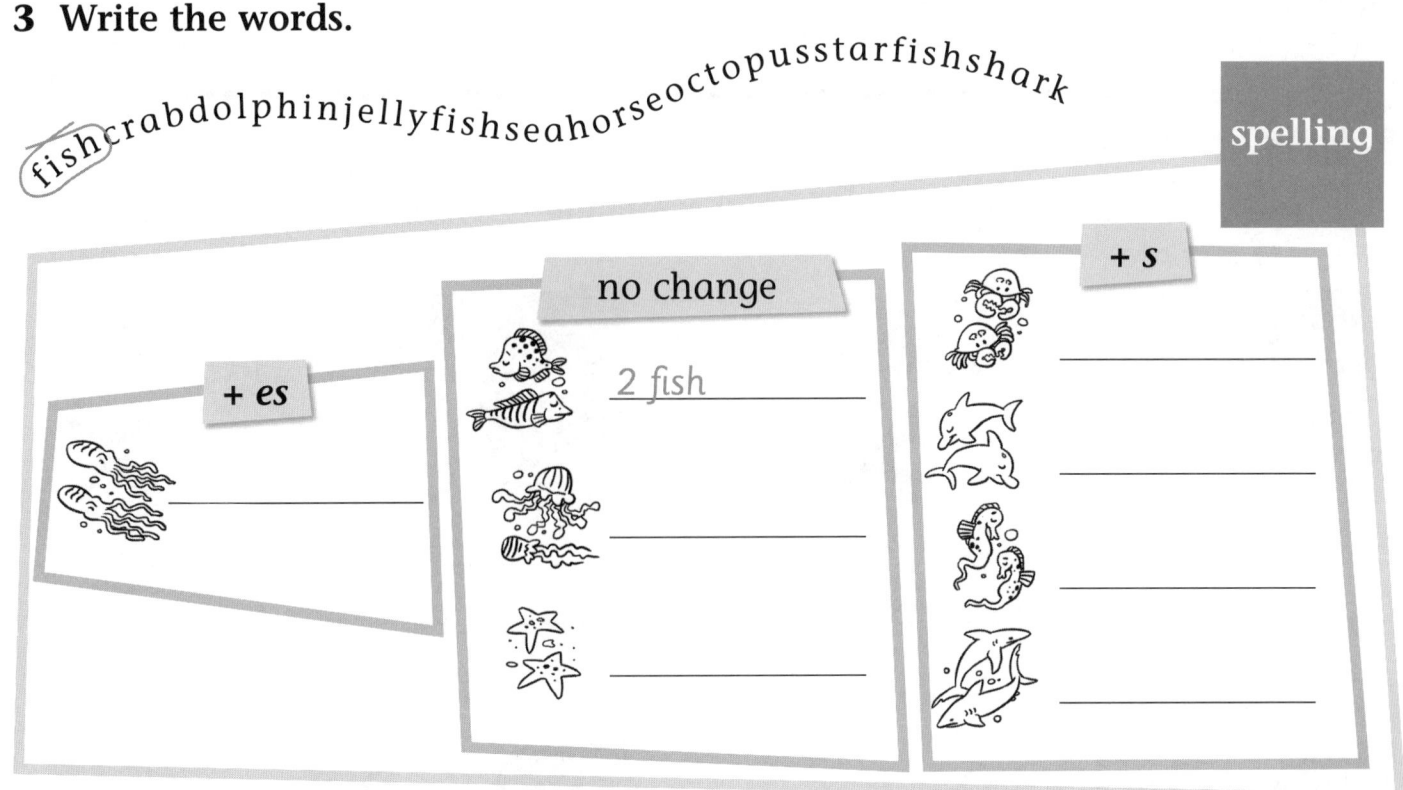

fish crab dolphin jellyfish seahorse octopus starfish shark

spelling

+ es

no change

2 fish

_____

_____

+ s

_____

_____

_____

_____

4 Look and complete.

This is a drawing of Water World. There are 2 _dolphins_ between the rocks. There are 6 _____ next to the rocks. There are 4 _____ under a dolphin. There's an _____ in a cave. There are 3 _____ behind the rocks. There are 3 _____ and 1 small _____ in front of the rock.

Spelling: Plurals ◆ There are 2 seahorses.

Unit 8

I saw an octopus. I didn't see a shark.

5 Look and write sentences.

saw   didn't see   went   didn't go   had   didn't have

1. He saw a shark.
   He didn't see a starfish.

2. _____
   _____

3. _____
   _____

4. _____
   _____

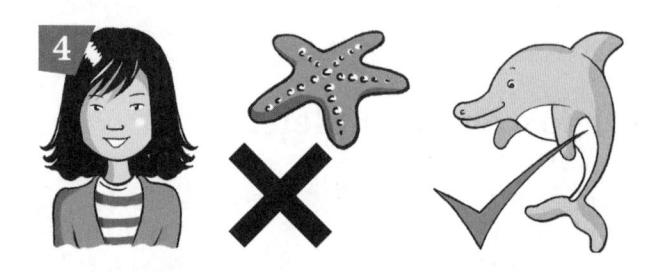

Did you go to the beach? Yes, I did.
Did you have chips? No, I didn't.

6 Make questions.

1 go did you beach to the?
   Did you go to the beach?

2 you did swimming go?
   _____

3 did see you octopus an?
   _____

4 to the did you go park?
   _____

5 a did sandwich have you?
   _____

6 have did an ice you cream?
   _____

76 Unit 8   I didn't see a sahrk. Did you see a crab?

7 Listen and tick ✓ or cross ✗. 2.45

I had a great weekend!

8 Read. Complete the dialogue. Then say.

Archie had a great weekend. He went to the beach and it was very hot!
He went swimming in the sea, and saw lots of beautiful fish. He saw some crabs, too!
He didn't have fish and chips but he had an ice cream. It was a great weekend.

Luke:	<u>Did you have a good weekend?</u> (have a good weekend)
Archie:	<u>Yes, I did.</u>
Luke:	_____? (go to the beach)
Archie:	_____
Luke:	_____? (go swimming)
Archie:	_____
Luke:	_____? (see any crabs)
Archie:	_____
Luke:	_____? (have fish and chips)
Archie:	_____
Luke:	_____? (have an ice cream)
Archie:	_____

◆ Did you see a shark? No, I didn't.

Unit 8 — 77

9 Listen to the story again. 2.43

10 Write the words in groups.

a starfish   pasta   a crab   chicken and chips   strawberry
a jellyfish   fish and chips   a fish   vanilla

an octopus

egg and chips

chocolate

11 Choose words and complete the playscript. Act.

Archie: We went to Water World. We had a great time!

Mum: What did you see?

Archie: I saw _____, _____ and _____!

Molly: And Coco saw the _____ too.

Jazmin: At lunchtime we had _____ … and we all had a _____ ice cream.

Molly: But Coco wanted to eat the _____ …

Finn: And she fell in!

Molly: Coco was a star! She played with the _____!

Finn: And at the end of the show she had _____ for lunch. She liked the _____!

78 Unit 8

Story language

12 Read and complete.

souvenirs   fruit   play   sail   postcards   skateboarding   chips   animals

Come to the Adventure Camp...

At the Adventure Camp you can see a lake and trees, birds and other wild _____ . At the Adventure Camp you can go _____ or rollerblading. You can learn how to row and _____ . You can meet new friends!

Look what you can do if you come to the Adventure Camp!

At The Adventure Camp you can _____ with your friends. You can learn new sports and activities. _____

In the The Adventure Camp Shop you can buy _____ and _____ .

In the The Adventure Camp Café we have delicous hot and cold food for you! You can eat sandwiches and _____ , sausages and _____ .

Come to the Adventure Camp and have fun!

13 Write a leaflet for a wildlife park or a water park. PMB page 42

What can you see?
What can you do?
What can you learn about?
What can you buy?
What can you eat?

Leaflets   Unit 8   79

14 Read and correct. Then listen and check. 🔊 2.46

1 We're going to the park, hurray!
2 We're going to the pool!
3 Let's pack our bus, what do we need?
4 Shorts and towels and lots of trees,
5 And games to play for you and she,
6 And lots of water, yes, yes cheese!
7 We're going to the shop, hurray!
8 We're going to the school!

— Fish —

15 Write the words.

sea　　deep　　river　　shallow　　lake　　surface　　bottom

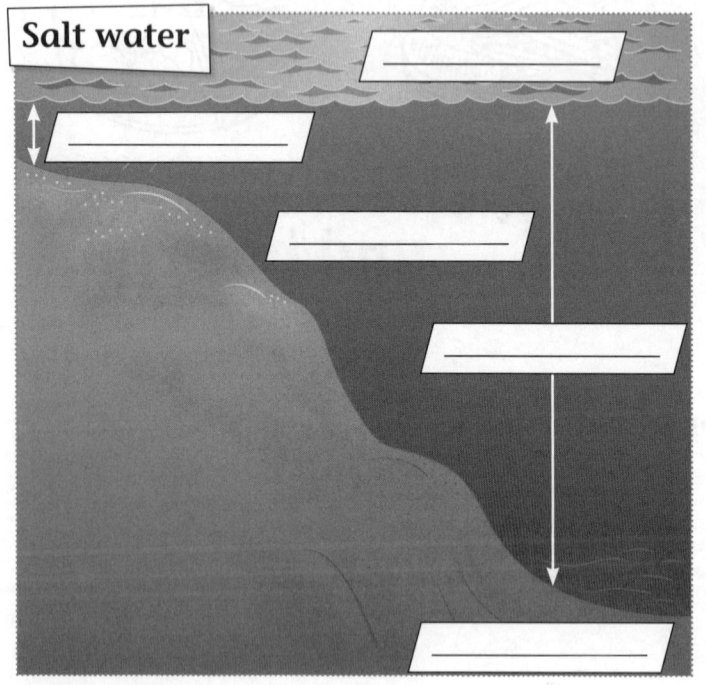

Salt water

Fresh water

Fish

16 Label the fish.

ray   cod   trout   sardine   pike

Salt water

Fresh water

17 Read and complete.

rivers   saltwater   bottom   freshwater   surface   the sea

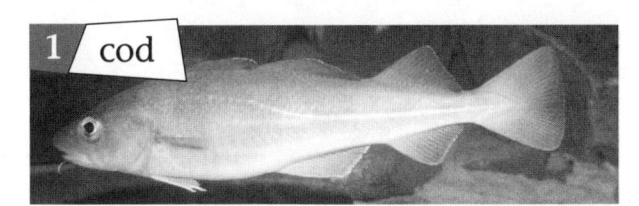

1 cod

1 This fish is a _____ fish.
   It lives in _____.
   It lives near the _____.

2 pike

2 This fish is a _____ fish.
   It lives in _____.
   It lives near the _____.

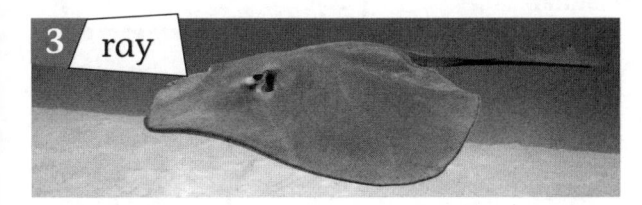

3 ray

3 This fish is a _____ fish.
   It lives in _____.
   It lives near the _____.

4 trout

4 This fish is a _____ fish.
   It lives in _____.
   It lives near the _____.

Science

Unit 8 | 81

18 Say. Write the words in the correct box.

house   scared   cake   cow   fair   snake

[aʊ]
mouse
_____
_____

[eɪ]
shake
_____
_____

[eə]
stairs
_____
_____

19 Write the words. What's the secret word?

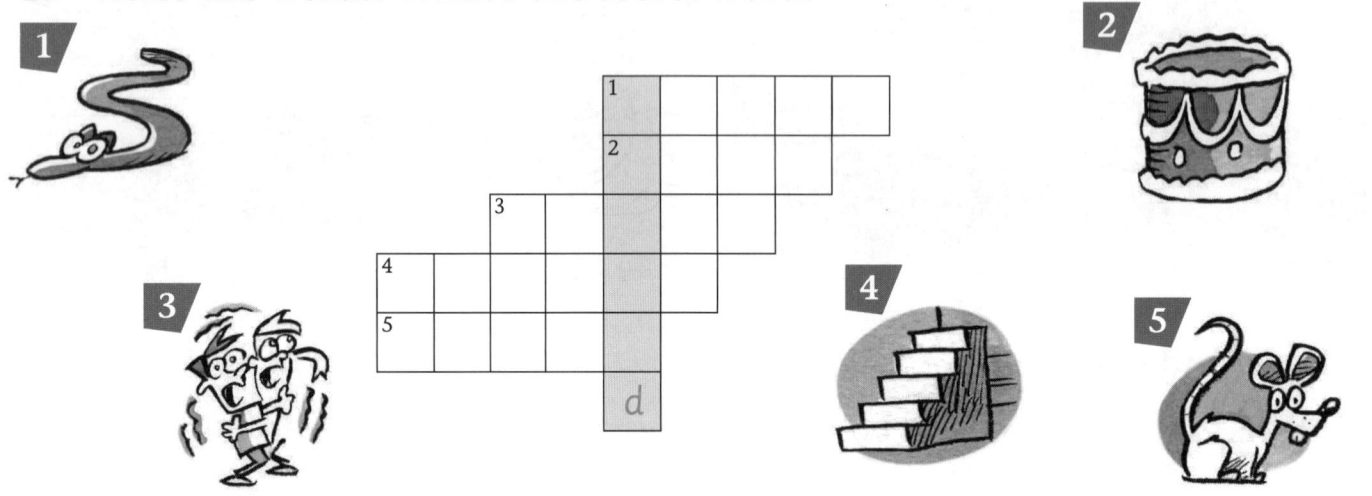

d

The secret word is _____

20 Look at the unit again. What can you do? Think and colour.

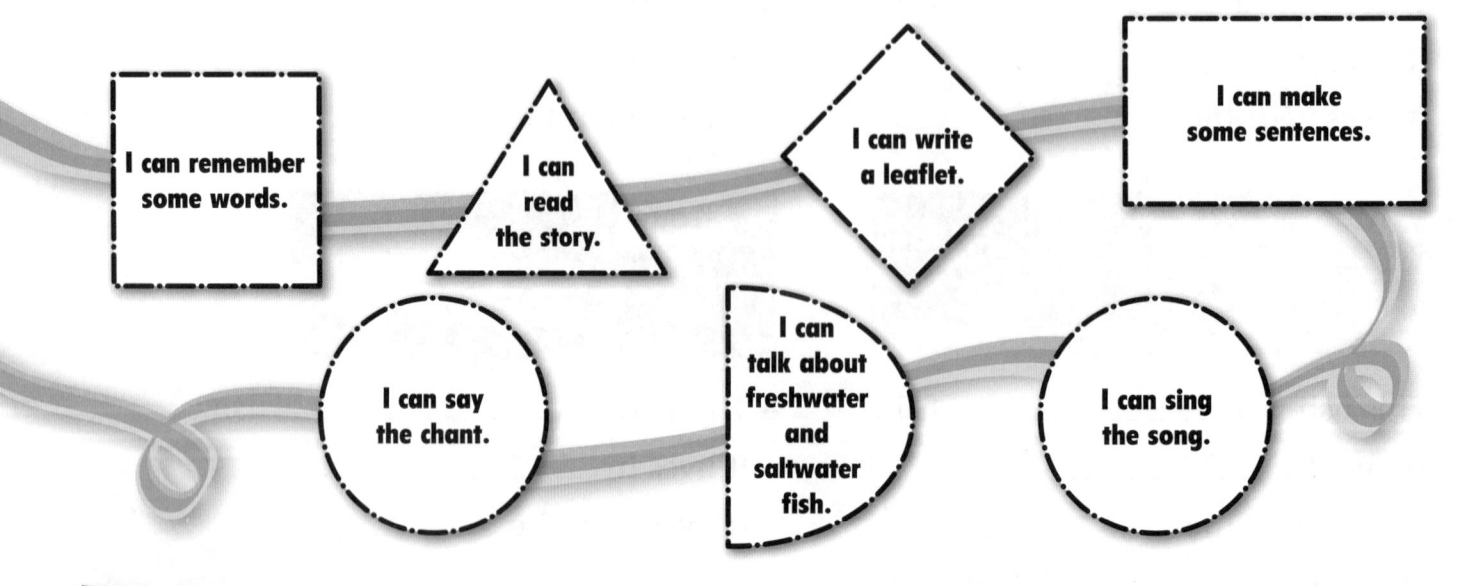

I can remember some words.

I can read the story.

I can write a leaflet.

I can make some sentences.

I can say the chant.

I can talk about freshwater and saltwater fish.

I can sing the song.

82 Unit 8   Pronunciation [aʊ] [eɪ] and [eə]   Review of the unit

Show what you know!

1 Find the words.

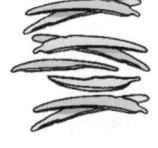

a	h	d	e	p	u	a	t	j	i	g	v	o
n	s	e	a	h	o	r	s	e	u	d	f	c
d	b	f	e	u	m	e	b	l	c	s	v	t
h	r	o	l	i	a	o	e	l	x	h	e	o
e	o	i	g	d	t	u	a	y	e	e	v	p
l	b	p	v	e	h	e	n	f	k	l	o	u
f	u	j	g	e	s	t	s	i	c	l	a	s
e	d	a	t	g	r	y	p	s	f	e	k	h
k	i	w	u	s	p	u	e	h	h	a	v	l
e	t	o	k	u	h	w	a	k	i	a	o	m
j	a	s	t	r	o	n	a	u	t	y	r	t
c	h	c	t	o	o	t	h	a	c	h	e	k
r	d	t	e	g	i	i	w	r	b	r	n	g

2 Make questions and answers.

1. did | to Water World | you | go | ?

    _____

2. did. | yes, | we

    _____

3. you | an octopus | see | did | ?

    _____

4. didn't. | no, | we | saw | a shark. | we

    _____

5. did | fish and chips | you | have | ? | we | did. | yes,

    _____

Revision

9 Technology

1 Number the pictures. Then write.

1 keyboard   2 mouse   3 text message   4 screen
5 memory stick   6 camera   7 laptop

Computer	Mobile phone

2 What does he need? Listen and tick ✓ or cross ✗. 3.3

84 Unit 9   Electrical items   I need …

3 What do they need at the club? Read and tick ✓.

> I went to the shop to buy a new computer. We need a new computer at the club. A normal desktop computer, not a laptop. We need a mouse and a keyboard too. And we need a big screen. We don't need a memory stick, but the shop assistant gave me one. When you buy a computer, the shop gives you a free mobile. We don't need it at the club, but the children like it. It has a camera so you can send text messages with a photo.

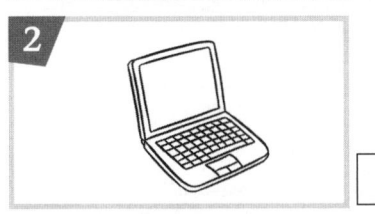

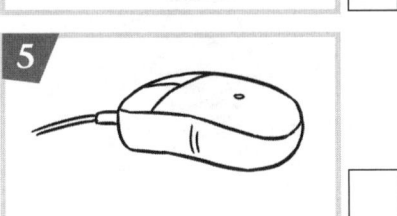

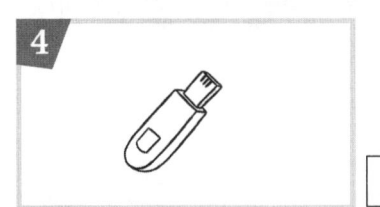

4 Write the words.   spelling

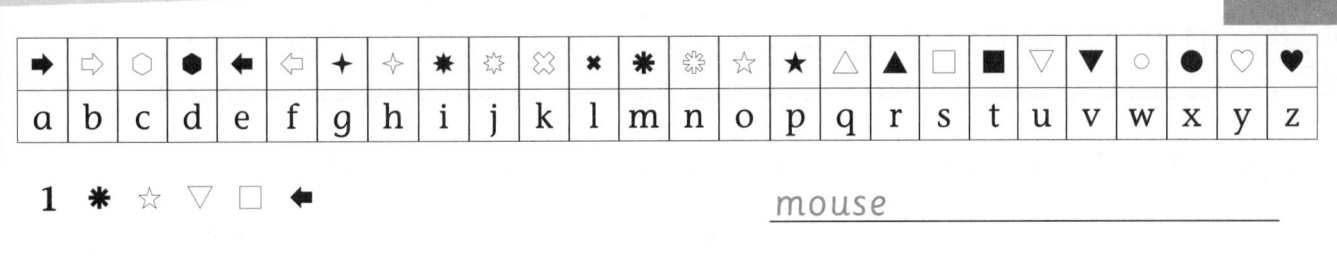

1. mouse
2. keyboard
3. memory stick
4. mobile phone
5. text message
6. computer

◆ We need a computer. We don't need a mobile.   ■ Spelling: Technology

He wanted the computer . He didn't want the TV .

5 Listen and look. Then write sentences. 3.6

opened   didn't open   wanted   didn't want   stayed   didn't stay

1 He didn't open the door.
2 _____
3 _____
4 _____
5 _____
6 _____

Did you go to the park ? Yes, I did . No, I didn't .

6 Listen. Then look and write the questions. Say. 3.7

Luke: What did you do at the weekend, Finn?
  a Did you go to the park?

Finn: Yes, I did. It was great.

Luke: b _____?
Finn: No, I didn't. It was too cold.

Luke: c _____?
Finn: Yes, I did. We played in the park. What about you?
  d _____?

Luke: Yes, I did. I watched a good film.

86 Unit 9   He wanted the computer. He didn't want the phone.

7 Look and write questions. Then ask your friend the questions.

Did you go to the park last weekend?

Yes, I did.

1 <u>Did you go to the park last weekend?</u>

2 _____

3 _____

4 _____

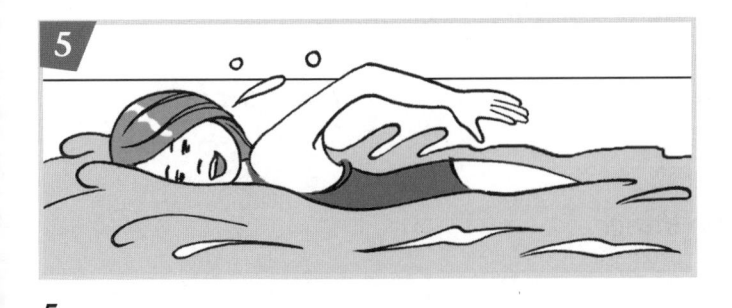

5 _____

6 _____

8 Write about your friend's weekend.

Last weekend my friend _____

Did you go to the park? Yes, I did.

Unit 9 **87**

9 Listen to the story again. 3.4

10 Write the words in groups.

mobile   on Saturday   laptop   great
incredible   door   hockey   on Sunday   screen

football   yesterday   computer

window   fantastic

11 Choose words and complete the playscript. Act.

Reporter:	So tell us – what happened _____?
Archie:	_____ we had a great day. We played _____.
Molly:	Then we had some fireworks.
Archie:	But Coco was scared and went into the club.
Jazmin:	Then a burglar opened the _____ and went in. He wanted the new _____.
Archie:	We didn't see or hear anything.
Molly:	But then he fell over Coco…
Jazmin:	We all chased the burglar.
Jazmin:	Then we got him! He fell in the goal!
Archie:	Yes – goal!!
Reporter:	Well done! You saved the Incredible Club! You really are _____ !
Kids:	Hurray!

12 Read and write A or B.

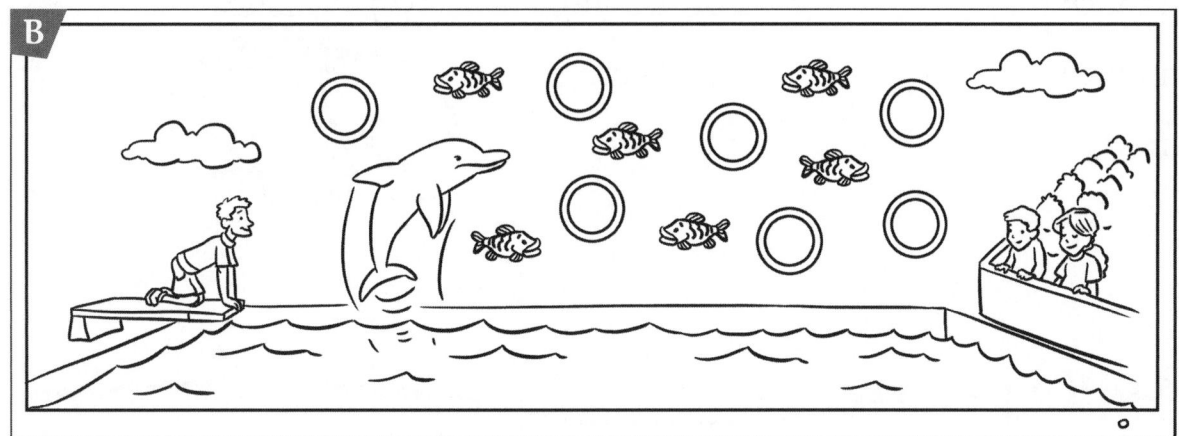

A

B

1 You must jump over the canyon. — A
2 When you catch a fish you get a point and more energy.
3 Be careful of the snakes and spiders. They want to catch you!
4 You mustn't touch the bees.
5 You must jump and catch fish.
6 When you catch a ring you get a point.
7 You are a dolphin.
8 You are a stunt bike rider.
9 When you drop a ring you lose a point and you lose some energy.
10 You can eat the chocolate bars for more energy.
11 You must catch the eggs. Lots of eggs!
12 If you fall in the canyon, the game is over.

13 Draw a game and write instructions. PMB page 47

Instructions

Unit 9

14 Read and match. Then listen and check. 3.8

1 Keep in touch   a not that hard.
2 Keep in touch   b from home!
3 Keep in touch   c by phone,
4 It's really   d by email,
5 Keep in touch   e by letter,
6 Keep in touch   f by visiting,
7 Keep in touch   g by texting,
8 You're never far   h by card,

Sending messages

15 Write the words.

flags   smoke   horse   drums   Morse code   pigeon

1 _____
2 _____
3 _____
4 _____
5 _____
6 _____

90   Unit 9   Keeping in touch   Types of messages

Sending messages

16 Write sentences.

1. He's sending a message with flags.

17 Can you read the message? Write the answer.

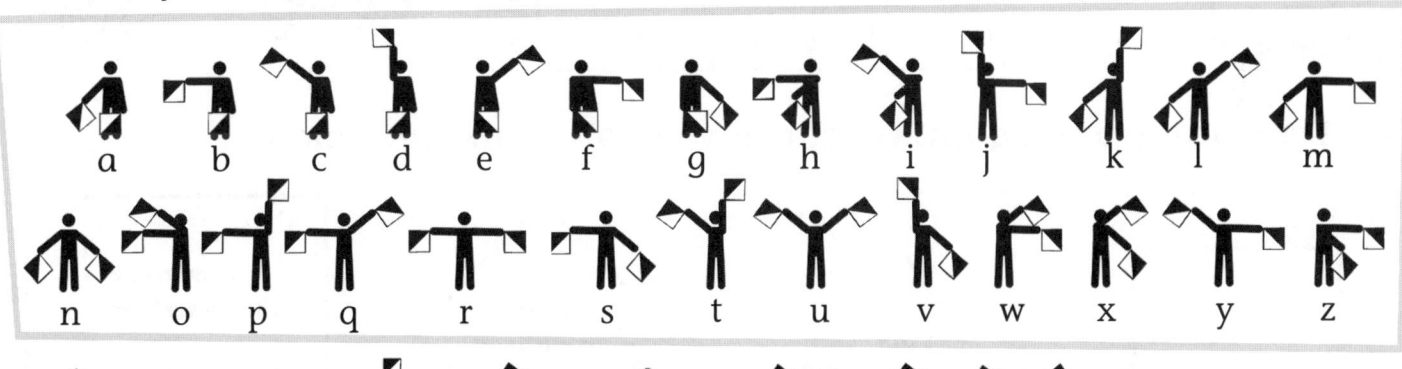

18 Say. Write the words in the correct box. Then find the words.

laughed   started   jumped   skipped   turned   exploded

d
played
_____
_____

ɪd
wanted
_____
_____

t
danced
_____
_____

d	r	I	w	s	t	h	o	j	k	e
a	s	t	a	r	t	e	d	g	e	x
f	k	f	n	o	g	r	g	q	f	p
n	i	s	t	u	r	n	e	d	I	l
l	p	w	e	x	o	f	r	o	z	o
a	p	p	d	a	n	c	e	d	x	d
u	e	c	l	t	v	s	c	b	h	e
g	d	q	y	a	d	b	a	i	u	d
h	w	s	c	r	y	f	f	s	v	e
e	c	j	u	m	p	e	d	c	t	w
d	x	q	e	u	z	t	d	q	v	k

19 Look at the unit again. What can you do? Think and colour.

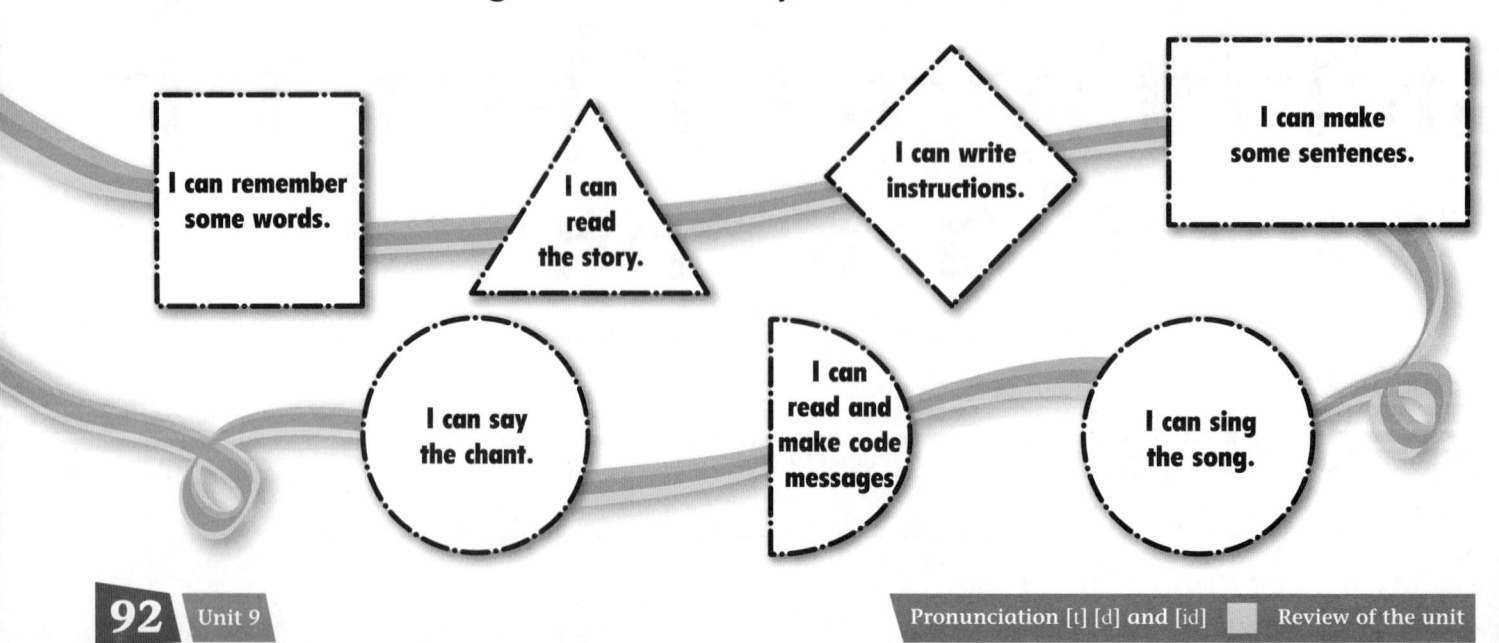

- I can remember some words.
- I can read the story.
- I can write instructions.
- I can make some sentences.
- I can say the chant.
- I can read and make code messages.
- I can sing the song.

Show what you know!

1 Look at the Class Book. Find the page.

1 Coco plays with the dolphin. _____
2 The children are arriving at the Adventure Camp. _page 3_
3 Finn's dad is in the school. _____
4 The goat escapes. _____
5 The children are at a museum. _____
6 There are lots of road signs. _____
7 Eve wants to buy a new mobile phone. _____
8 Coco catches the mouse. _____
9 Eve feels dizzy. _____

2 Write more words.

On the road
traffic lights

At school
Maths

Underwater life
seahorse

Technology
mobile phone

Revision

Children around the world — My country

1 Listen and draw. 🔊 3.22

a.

b.

2 Read, choose and write.

> This is Turkey in winter.
> There are lots of black clouds.
> There are some clouds, but not many.
> I'm wearing a cap, a jacket and jeans.
>
> This is Thailand in summer.
> It's windy and cold.
> It's raining, but it's very hot.
> I've got an umbrella.

a.

b.

_____   _____
_____   _____
_____   _____
_____   _____
_____   _____

Children around the world: My journey to school

1 Listen and number. Then match. 3.24

a **I ride my bike to school.**
b **I walk to school.**
c **I take the school bus.**
d **I go to school by car.**

2 Read and write the name.

a Jacob's journey
b Brooke's journey

1 It's very noisy, but it's very fast. _____
2 I meet all my friends so I love it! _____
3 I sit behind my Mum. _____
4 It stops in front of my house. _____
5 I sit at the front with my best friends. _____
6 We can travel off the roads. _____

Children around the world

My school

1 Listen and write the names. 🔊 3.26

| 1 | Jacob | 2 | Brooke | 3 | Sunee | 4 | Kemal |

a Name _____

	Monday
8.30	English
9.30	I.T.
10.30	Maths
11.30	P.E.
12.30	Lunch

b Name _____

	Monday
9.00	D&T
9.40	Drama
10.20	Science
11.00	P.E.

c Name _____

	Monday
8.45	Science
9.30	English
10.15	Drama
11.00	Maths
11.45	Lunch

d Name _____

	Monday
9.00	Maths
9.45	D&T
10.30	I.T.
11.15	Science
12.00	Lunch

2 Look and write.

1. I always go to the cinema at the weekends. My favourite subject is Drama. I want to be…

2. I love drawing and painting. I always go to the galleries on holiday. I want to be…

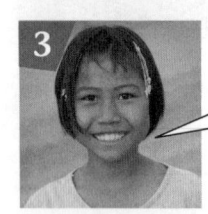

3. I like all my subjects. After school, I help other children in my class with homework. I want to be…

4. My favourite subjects are I.T. and Science. In the evenings, I always watch the stars and the moon. I want to be…